Conquer AZ-305: Architecting Azure Like a Pro

Kameron Hussain and Frahaan Hussain

Published by Sonar Publishing, 2025.

CONQUER AZ-305: ARCHITECTING AZURE LIKE A PRO

First edition. May 25, 2025.

ISBN: 979-8231647781

Written by Kameron Hussain and Frahaan Hussain.

Conquer AZ-305: Architecting Azure Like a Pro

First Edition

Preface

Welcome to the first edition of *Conquer AZ-305: Architecting Azure Like a Pro*. This book is designed for cloud professionals and aspiring Azure Solutions Architects who are preparing for the Microsoft AZ-305 certification exam: *Designing Microsoft Azure Infrastructure Solutions*. The AZ-305 is a capstone certification in the Microsoft Certified: Azure Solutions Architect Expert track, and it tests a candidate's ability to design cloud and hybrid solutions that run on Microsoft Azure.

As cloud architecture becomes a critical role in modern IT strategy, professionals must go beyond simply deploying services. They must understand how to design secure, scalable, high-performing, and cost-optimized architectures that meet complex business requirements. This book is built to bridge the gap between theory and implementation, combining exam-focused study material with deep architectural insights and practical guidance.

Each chapter is aligned with the skills measured in the AZ-305 exam blueprint, offering comprehensive coverage of identity, governance, storage, networking, compute, application design, and business continuity. Additionally, you'll find discussions on decision-making trade-offs, architectural patterns, and best practices—providing real-world context for the certification content.

Whether you're an experienced cloud architect looking to validate your skills or a seasoned IT pro transitioning to cloud-native design, this book is structured to help you succeed:

- **Chapters 1 through 6** provide technical depth, architectural patterns, and real-world examples for each AZ-305 domain.

- **Chapter 7** is your exam preparation hub with question walkthroughs, time management strategies, and study plans.

- **Chapter 8** offers reference material including glossaries, API samples, and project scenarios to reinforce practical learning.

Throughout the book, examples and sample architectures are inspired by enterprise scenarios across industries such as finance, healthcare, retail, and SaaS. As Azure continues to evolve rapidly, we've made sure to focus on enduring architectural principles and Azure-native services that are core to Microsoft's cloud ecosystem.

Your journey to becoming a Microsoft Certified Azure Solutions Architect begins here. Let's conquer AZ-305 together.

Table of Contents

Chapter 1: Introduction to AZ-305 and the Azure Architect Role

Understanding the AZ-305 Certification Path

THE AZ-305: DESIGNING Microsoft Azure Infrastructure Solutions certification is a pivotal milestone for any cloud professional pursuing the Microsoft Certified: Azure Solutions Architect Expert designation. Unlike foundational certifications like AZ-900 or administrator-level credentials such as AZ-104, AZ-305 focuses exclusively on high-level design and architectural decisions.

Achieving this certification demonstrates your ability to translate business requirements into secure, scalable, and reliable Azure solutions. It is not merely about knowing individual Azure services—it's about integrating them coherently into cloud architectures that meet performance, security, and compliance objectives.

Certification Prerequisites

TO EARN THE *Azure Solutions Architect Expert* credential, you must pass two exams:

1. **AZ-104**: Microsoft Azure Administrator
2. **AZ-305**: Designing Microsoft Azure Infrastructure Solutions

This dual-requirement emphasizes the dual nature of the architect role: deep administrative knowledge and broad architectural vision. You are expected to understand the implementation details (from AZ-104) and the design-level decision-making (from AZ-305).

Candidate Profile

MICROSOFT DEFINES THE ideal AZ-305 candidate as someone with:

• Advanced experience in IT operations including networking, virtualization, identity, security, business continuity, disaster recovery, data platform, budgeting, and governance

• Deep understanding of Azure services and workloads

• Familiarity with Azure CLI, PowerShell, ARM templates, Bicep, and Azure Portal

• Experience in DevOps processes and continuous integration and deployment (CI/CD) practices

In practice, this means the AZ-305 candidate is someone who can:

• Lead cloud transformation initiatives

• Communicate trade-offs to stakeholders

• Design systems that satisfy both IT governance and developer agility

Exam Focus Areas

THE AZ-305 EXAM IS organized into four functional groups:

1. **Design Identity, Governance, and Monitoring Solutions**
2. **Design Data Storage Solutions**
3. **Design Business Continuity Solutions**
4. **Design Infrastructure Solutions**

Each area maps directly to job functions expected of an Azure Solutions Architect. Candidates must be able to evaluate design options and make justifiable recommendations across all these domains.

Study Path Recommendations

A SMART STUDY PLAN for AZ-305 should include:

• **Deep dives into architectural decision points** — When would you use Azure Files over Blob Storage? What's the best way to enforce policy across multiple subscriptions?

• **Architecture scenario walkthroughs** — Simulate real-world situations: A global ecommerce app needing multi-region resiliency and latency optimization.

• **Azure documentation exploration** — This is not a test of memorization. Microsoft expects familiarity with architecture center resources, reference architectures, and service limits.

• **Hands-on experience in the portal and CLI** — Knowing how to design a virtual network is one thing; building it with route tables, subnets, and NSGs is another.

• **Mock tests** — These solidify retention, improve time management, and reduce exam-day anxiety.

Sample Learning Plan (8 Weeks)

Week	Topics	Activities
1	AZ-305 Overview, Identity Design	Microsoft Learn, create/test AAD tenants
2	RBAC, Governance, Policy	Practice Blueprints, define management groups
3	Monitoring and Logging	Explore Log Analytics queries, create workbooks
4	Storage Design	Build Blob lifecycle rules, use AzCopy and Storage Explorer
5	Backup and DR, Business Continuity	Test Azure Backup, simulate failovers with ASR
6	Network and Compute Design	Deploy VNets, NSGs, VMs, containers with scaling settings
7	Application Architecture (AKS, Functions, API Mgmt)	Build a Function App, simulate AKS workloads
8	Final Review and Mock Exams	Take full-length exams, review gaps

Tips for Success

- **Think architecturally**: This isn't a test of "how," it's a test of "why."
- **Understand trade-offs**: Every decision has implications for cost, performance, security, and manageability.
- **Focus on Azure-native tools**: While third-party integrations are valid, the exam expects Azure-centric solutions.

Real-World Example: Design Trade-off

LET'S IMAGINE A RETAIL company planning to store large amounts of customer order data, which must be retained for 7 years and occasionally queried for reports.

You're asked: **Which Azure storage option should be used?**

- **Option A**: Azure SQL Database
- **Option B**: Azure Blob Storage with Archive Tier
- **Option C**: Azure Data Lake Gen2
- **Option D**: Azure Table Storage

Answer and Reasoning:

- SQL Database is expensive for long-term archival and not optimized for large unstructured datasets.
- Table Storage is cost-effective but lacks rich query support.
- Data Lake is powerful but may be overkill and more expensive than needed.
- **Blob Storage with Archive Tier** is best: lowest cost for long-term archival, and rehydration supports occasional queries.

This is the kind of scenario you'll encounter. Not how to configure Blob Storage, but *why* to choose it over other options based on requirements.

Resources for Further Study

- **Microsoft Learn – AZ-305 Learning Path**
- **Azure Architecture Center – Reference Architectures**

- **Exam Skills Outline PDF** (from Microsoft)
- **Pluralsight/ACloudGuru Courses**
- **GitHub Repos with Sample Azure Infrastructure as Code**
- **Official Azure Docs – Service Limits and Best Practices**

Summary

UNDERSTANDING THE AZ-305 exam path is the first step in mastering Azure architecture. This certification demands not just technical knowledge, but strategic thinking and real-world architectural fluency. By focusing on scenario-based reasoning, trade-offs, and best practices, you'll be well-equipped to pass the exam and perform effectively in real Azure projects.

This section set the stage for the chapters ahead—where each topic is covered with detailed explanations, real-world patterns, and exam-aligned guidance. Let's move forward and begin designing identity, governance, and monitoring solutions in Chapter 2.

Overview of Azure Solutions Architect Responsibilities

THE ROLE OF AN AZURE Solutions Architect encompasses far more than deploying cloud infrastructure or configuring services. It requires the ability to translate high-level business goals into technical architectures that are scalable, secure, cost-efficient, and operationally robust. The architect acts as the bridge between stakeholders—including business executives, developers, security teams, and operations—and the Azure platform.

This section delves into the end-to-end responsibilities of an Azure Solutions Architect, aligned with the expectations set by Microsoft and the realities of working in complex enterprise environments. These responsibilities span five critical domains:

1. **Requirement Gathering and Solution Planning**
2. **Designing End-to-End Azure Architectures**
3. **Governance, Security, and Compliance**
4. **Operational and Cost Optimization Planning**
5. **Stakeholder Communication and Documentation**

Requirement Gathering and Solution Planning

BEFORE ANY AZURE SERVICE is provisioned, the architect must engage in deep discovery. This is where the technical vision is aligned with business strategy. Key responsibilities in this phase include:

• **Identifying business objectives**: Understanding whether the goal is to reduce on-premises footprint, enable global expansion, support a SaaS product launch, or improve disaster recovery.

• **Translating non-functional requirements (NFRs)**: Such as availability, latency, compliance, data sovereignty, and support SLAs.

• **Assessing existing environments**: This may involve reviewing current infrastructure (on-prem or cloud), integration points, and performance bottlenecks.

• **Prioritizing outcomes**: Some projects prioritize time-to-market, while others value operational stability or cost savings above all.

Sample Planning Matrix:

Requirement Area	Input Example	Architectural Implication
Availability	99.99% uptime SLA for e-commerce API	Requires multi-zone deployment and load balancing
Latency	<100ms response in Europe and Asia	Suggests regional pairing or CDN deployment
Security	Must meet ISO 27001, HIPAA, GDPR	Mandates encryption, audit logs, key management
Cost Constraint	Max £5,000/month operational cost	May influence compute size and PaaS adoption
Scalability	Support traffic spikes during holidays	Consider autoscaling AKS or serverless patterns

The architect must facilitate meetings, ask probing questions, and review documentation to ensure nothing critical is missed.

Designing End-to-End Azure Architectures

THE CORE DELIVERABLE for the Azure Solutions Architect is a comprehensive architectural blueprint. This design includes a layered approach that considers the entire application lifecycle and deployment topology.

Common Components of Azure Architectures

- **Compute Layer**:
    - Azure Virtual Machines
    - Azure App Service
    - Azure Kubernetes Service (AKS)

    - Azure Functions (serverless)

- **Data Layer:**
    - Azure SQL Database / Managed Instance
    - Cosmos DB (for global low-latency workloads)
    - Blob Storage / Data Lake Gen2
- **Integration Layer:**
    - API Management
    - Azure Logic Apps
    - Event Grid and Service Bus
- **Network and Security Layer:**
    - Virtual Networks, Subnets, NSGs
    - Azure Firewall, Private Endpoints, VPNs
    - Azure Front Door, Application Gateway
- **Management Layer:**
    - Azure Monitor
    - Log Analytics
    - Azure Policy / Blueprints
    - Resource Graph, ARM templates, and Bicep

Reference Design Sample

HERE'S A PSEUDOCODE representation of a high-availability web architecture using Bicep:

```
resource vnet 'Microsoft.Network/virtualNetworks@2022-01-01' = {

name: 'prod-vnet'

location: resourceGroup().location

properties: {

addressSpace: {

addressPrefixes: ['10.0.0.0/16']

}

subnets: [

{

name: 'web-subnet'

properties: {

addressPrefix: '10.0.1.0/24'

}

}

]

}

}
```

```
resource appServicePlan 'Microsoft.Web/serverfarms@2022-03-01'
= {

name: 'asp-prod'

location: resourceGroup().location

sku: {

name: 'P1v2'

tier: 'PremiumV2'

}

}

resource app 'Microsoft.Web/sites@2022-03-01' = {

name: 'myapp-prod'

location: resourceGroup().location

properties: {

serverFarmId: appServicePlan.id

}

}
```

This kind of IaC deployment is common for automating repeatable environments with governed templates.

Governance, Security, and Compliance

AZURE ARCHITECTS MUST embed governance and compliance controls into the architecture from day one. Security must not be bolted on after the fact—it must be designed into the system.

Governance Activities

- **Management Group Hierarchy Design**: Organize subscriptions by function, compliance boundary, or business unit.
- **Policy and Initiative Assignment**: Enforce controls such as restricting VM SKUs, requiring tags, or enforcing region limits.
- **Blueprint Composition**: Preconfigure environments with RBAC, policies, ARM templates, and resource locks.

Security Considerations

- **Zero Trust Network Model**: Assume breach, enforce least privilege, monitor continuously.
- **Encryption**:
    - At-rest with customer-managed keys (CMK) using Azure Key Vault
    - In-transit via HTTPS/TLS 1.2+ only endpoints
- **Identity Controls**:
    - Enforce Azure AD MFA
    - Use Conditional Access policies
    - Grant app permissions via Managed Identities

Compliance Framework Mapping

Compliance Requirement	Azure Toolset
HIPAA	Key Vault, Azure Policy, Azure Monitor, PIM
ISO 27001	Microsoft Defender for Cloud, Audit Logs
GDPR	Data classification, DSR automation, region control

THE ARCHITECT IS ACCOUNTABLE for documenting how compliance is maintained and for collaborating with legal/ compliance departments.

Operational and Cost Optimization Planning

A WELL-ARCHITECTED solution must also be operable and financially sustainable. The Azure Solutions Architect must balance performance and availability against budget constraints.

Cost Optimization Strategies

- **Right-size compute**: Use Azure Advisor recommendations and performance metrics.
- **Choose PaaS when possible**: Offload operational overhead.
- **Enable auto-scaling**: Prevent over-provisioning during off-peak hours.
- **Apply Reservations or Savings Plans**: Commit to 1–3 year plans to reduce cost by up to 72%.

- **Leverage Cost Management + Billing**: Monitor spend by tags, departments, and subscriptions.

Operational Design Areas

- **Monitoring Strategy**:
  - Application Insights for application-level telemetry
  - Azure Monitor Alerts for autoscaling and incident detection
  - Log Analytics workbooks for dashboards
- **Business Continuity Planning**:
  - Backup policies
  - Geo-redundant storage
  - Active-Active architecture for mission-critical apps
- **Deployability and DevOps**:
  - CI/CD pipelines with GitHub Actions or Azure DevOps
  - Blue/green or canary deployment strategies
  - Infrastructure as Code for repeatable environments

The Azure Well-Architected Framework should guide operational excellence across these pillars.

Stakeholder Communication and Documentation

A CRUCIAL PART OF THE architect's role is articulating the rationale behind design decisions to both technical and non-technical stakeholders. The ability to communicate clearly is often as important as technical accuracy.

Deliverables Often Owned by the Architect

- **Solution Architecture Diagrams**: Logical, network, and data flow representations
- **Decision Logs**: Capturing alternatives considered and the reasoning behind final choices
- **Security and Compliance Mapping**: A mapping between architecture and framework (e.g., NIST, ISO)
- **Cost Model Forecasts**: Estimated monthly spend, cost per environment, per feature
- **Deployment Playbooks**: Step-by-step operational guides for environment setup or recovery

Communication Techniques

- **Executive Briefings**: Focus on business impact, cost, and risk mitigation.
- **Technical Workshops**: Dive deep into platform choices, redundancy models, and integration approaches.
- **Cross-team Collaboration**: Work closely with developers, DBAs, security officers, and finance analysts.

Good architects not only deliver scalable cloud infrastructure—they ensure everyone understands its value and operation.

Summary

THE AZURE SOLUTIONS Architect is a strategic role requiring expertise in cloud architecture, governance, security, cost optimization, and stakeholder communication. Architects must stay ahead of cloud service evolution, remain fluent in best practices, and be capable of aligning diverse technical solutions with strategic business outcomes.

While the tools and services will continue to evolve, the core responsibility remains: delivering Azure solutions that are secure, resilient, and cost-effective while meeting real-world business needs.

In the next section, we'll explore the key skills and knowledge areas that are critical to succeed both in the AZ-305 exam and in real-world architect roles.

Key Skills and Knowledge Areas for Exam Success

SUCCESS IN THE AZ-305 certification exam requires a combination of deep technical expertise, architectural thinking, decision-making skills, and the ability to connect business objectives with the right Azure services. The exam does not test rote memorization—it challenges candidates to demonstrate applied knowledge across a variety of solution scenarios.

This section explores the essential competencies required to pass the exam and excel in a real-world Azure Solutions Architect role. These skill areas are grouped into the following categories:

- Foundational Azure Knowledge
- Solution Design Skills
- Security, Governance, and Identity
- Networking and Infrastructure
- Storage and Data Solutions
- Monitoring and Business Continuity
- Integration and Application Design
- Cost Management and Optimization
- Hands-On Technical Proficiency

Foundational Azure Knowledge

AT THE CORE OF THE AZ-305 exam is the assumption that candidates already understand the foundational elements of Azure. These include:

- **Azure Resource Manager (ARM)**: Understand resource groups, tags, templates, locks, and scopes.
- **Azure CLI and PowerShell**: Know how to automate tasks, query resource status, and deploy templates.
- **Azure Subscription Hierarchy**:
    - Management Groups
    - Subscriptions
    - Resource Groups

  - Resources

- **Azure Regions and Availability Zones**: Know how geography affects service availability, compliance, and latency.
- **Deployment Models**:
  - ARM Templates
  - Bicep
  - Terraform (beneficial but not required)

You should be able to answer design-related questions such as:

"How would you structure your resource hierarchy to support a multi-department, multi-region architecture while enforcing global policies?"

This leads to designs involving management groups for departments, subscriptions per workload, and policy initiatives at various levels.

Solution Design Skills

PERHAPS THE MOST CRITICAL competency for AZ-305 is *architectural decision-making*. You need to weigh trade-offs and recommend the most appropriate service or pattern.

Example Scenario:

REQUIREMENT: Design a web application with variable traffic and minimal management overhead.

Solution:

- **Compute**: Azure App Service with autoscaling

- **Storage**: Blob Storage for static content
- **Security**: Azure Front Door with WAF
- **Monitoring**: Application Insights
- **CI/CD**: GitHub Actions with slot-based deployment

The ability to assemble such designs is fundamental. You must understand:

- Stateless vs stateful architectures
- Synchronous vs asynchronous workflows
- Batch vs stream processing
- Application layering and API gateway placement
- Multi-tier and microservices patterns

Security, Governance, and Identity

SECURITY AND GOVERNANCE are central pillars of the exam. Expect questions that test your ability to:

- Design Azure AD tenant structure for B2B or B2C scenarios
- Enforce identity protection with Conditional Access and MFA
- Apply RBAC at different scopes with least privilege access
- Implement Privileged Identity Management (PIM)
- Use Azure Policy to control service deployment and enforce compliance

Example Use Case: You need to restrict developers to only deploy certain VM SKUs and ensure all resources are tagged by environment.

Solution:

- Apply Azure Policy to restrict allowed SKUs:

```
{
"if": {
"field": "Microsoft.Compute/virtualMachines/sku.name",
"notIn": ["Standard_DS1_v2", "Standard_DS2_v2"]
},
"then": {
"effect": "deny"
}
}
```

- Enforce mandatory tags:
    - Create an initiative that audits or denies resource creation without environment and owner tags.

This combination of identity and policy control forms a secure, compliant deployment baseline.

Networking and Infrastructure

A SUBSTANTIAL PORTION of the exam focuses on infrastructure, particularly networking. Core topics include:

- Virtual Network (VNet) Design:
  - Subnet planning
  - IP address planning (CIDR ranges)
  - Route tables and peering
- Hybrid Networking:
  - VPN Gateway
  - ExpressRoute
  - Virtual WAN
- Network Security:
  - NSGs
  - Azure Firewall
  - Application Gateway WAF
  - Private Endpoints and Private Link
- Load Balancing:
  - Layer 4: Azure Load Balancer
  - Layer 7: Azure Application Gateway
  - Global: Azure Front Door and Traffic Manager

Example Design Decision:

Problem: You need to expose an internal web application securely to business partners with high availability.

Solution:

- Place app behind Application Gateway with WAF
- Use Private Link to keep backend traffic internal
- Set up B2B access with Azure AD and Conditional Access

You should be able to diagram and justify such a network design in detail, including DNS resolution, IP ranges, and HA failover.

Storage and Data Solutions

DESIGNING DATA STORAGE is a critical competency. You must be able to evaluate:

- **Blob Storage tiers**: Hot, Cool, Archive
- **Azure Files vs. Blob vs. Data Lake**
- **SQL vs NoSQL**: Azure SQL, Cosmos DB, Table Storage
- **Backup, Replication, and Redundancy**:
    - LRS, ZRS, GRS, RA-GRS
- **Encryption and access control**

Scenario: You must archive invoices for 10 years with minimal cost and retrieval requirements.

Solution:

- Use Blob Storage Archive tier

- Set lifecycle management policies to transition after 30 days

Additionally, Cosmos DB requires deep understanding for global-scale apps:

- Consistency levels (strong, bounded staleness, session, eventual)
- Partitioning strategies
- TTL and change feed use cases

Monitoring and Business Continuity

MONITORING, RECOVERY, and continuity strategies are extensively covered in AZ-305. Focus areas include:

- **Azure Monitor and Application Insights**:
    - Metric alerts
    - Custom telemetry
    - Dependency tracking
- **Log Analytics Queries (KQL)**:
    - Write queries to filter logs, track errors, detect anomalies
- **Azure Backup**:
    - VM, file, and SQL protection
    - Backup policies and retention
- **Azure Site Recovery (ASR)**:

    - Region-to-region VM replication
    - Failover/failback planning
- **Availability Zones and Regions**:
    - Deploying across zones and pairs for resiliency

Use Case:

Design a BCDR plan for an e-commerce site with 2-hour RTO and 15-minute RPO.

Architecture:

- Active/Passive deployment across paired regions
- GRS for storage
- ASR for VMs and critical stateful services
- Application Gateway with Front Door for traffic routing

Integration and Application Design

AS MODERN APPLICATIONS rely on complex integrations, you must understand:

- **API Management**:
    - Rate limits, subscriptions, key authentication
- **Azure Logic Apps**:
    - Workflow orchestration, connectors for SaaS
- **Event Grid and Service Bus**:

    - Event-driven design
    - Durable messaging
    - Dead-letter queues

- **Azure Functions and Durable Functions**

Scenario: You must build a scalable serverless solution that processes uploaded PDFs and sends notifications.

Design:

- Blob trigger Function processes the file
- Logic App sends email notification
- Cosmos DB stores metadata
- Service Bus queues failed uploads for retry

This demonstrates your ability to create loosely coupled, resilient architectures.

Cost Management and Optimization

ARCHITECTS MUST DESIGN with fiscal responsibility. Key tools and skills include:

- **Azure Pricing Calculator**: Model and compare costs
- **Cost Management + Billing** dashboards
- **Budgets and Alerts**
- **Tag-based cost tracking**
- **Reservations and Savings Plans**

Scenario: Your client's PaaS database cost has doubled unexpectedly.

Resolution:

- Use Cost Analysis to find out query volume spikes
- Apply scaling rules based on CPU/memory metrics
- Consider moving to Hyperscale or reserved instance

Optimizing for cost without sacrificing performance is a balancing act, and AZ-305 expects you to do this routinely.

Hands-On Technical Proficiency

THOUGH THE EXAM IS not lab-based, hands-on experience is indispensable. You should practice:

- **Deploying entire environments with Bicep or ARM**
- **Setting up policies, diagnostics, identity controls**
- **Simulating outages and failovers**
- **Running KQL queries in Log Analytics**
- **Testing Azure AD configurations for B2B/B2C**

Try to work through at least 2–3 full architecture builds end-to-end before taking the exam. These could include:

- A multi-tier web app with SQL back end
- A serverless workflow with Event Grid and Logic Apps
- A secure hybrid VNet with VPN and ExpressRoute
- A disaster recovery simulation using ASR and traffic routing

Summary

TO SUCCEED IN THE AZ-305 exam, you must go beyond surface-level familiarity. The exam demands breadth and depth—across Azure services, architectural patterns, security strategies, and governance controls.

Core competencies include:

- Decision-making based on trade-offs
- Designing for availability, performance, security, and cost
- Using Azure-native tools effectively
- Applying real-world patterns to scenario-based questions

In the next section, we'll explore how to use this book effectively to build a study routine, fill in skill gaps, and maximize your chances of passing AZ-305 on your first attempt.

How to Use This Book Effectively

THIS BOOK HAS BEEN designed not just as a study guide, but as a comprehensive reference manual for preparing for the AZ-305 exam and mastering Azure solution architecture. To gain the most from this resource, you must use it intentionally, with a focus on integration, practical application, and scenario-based learning. This section will outline strategies for using the book to maximize both your exam readiness and real-world capability.

Understand the Book's Structure

EACH CHAPTER IS STRUCTURED around the core domains tested in the AZ-305 certification exam:

- Identity, governance, and monitoring solutions
- Data storage solutions
- Business continuity and disaster recovery strategies
- Infrastructure and application design

Each chapter consists of multiple sub-sections that follow this format:

- **Conceptual Foundation**: Explanation of core Azure concepts
- **Use Cases and Scenarios**: Real-world examples and architectural decisions
- **Design Patterns and Trade-Offs**: Comparative discussions for selecting services
- **Best Practices**: Proven strategies drawn from field implementations
- **Exam Tips**: Highlighted points likely to appear in exam scenarios
- **Hands-On Practice (Optional)**: CLI, Bicep, ARM template, or PowerShell exercises

This layered approach ensures that you're not only learning *what* services exist, but *how* and *why* to use them in a practical solution.

Recommended Reading Paths

NOT ALL READERS APPROACH this book with the same background. The following reading paths are suggested depending on your current experience level and certification goals.

Path A: Administrator-to-Architect Transition

IF YOU ALREADY HOLD the AZ-104 (Azure Administrator Associate) certification:

1. Skim Chapter 1 to align with AZ-305 mindset
2. Focus deeply on Chapters 2, 4, and 6 (governance, DR, application architecture)
3. Use Chapter 5 to expand from operations to design
4. Use Chapter 7 to benchmark yourself with mock questions
5. Practice scenarios in Chapter 8.3 and 8.4

Path B: Cloud Beginner With Technical Background

1. Read Chapter 1 thoroughly to understand the certification roadmap
2. Move linearly through Chapters 2 to 6 without skipping subtopics
3. Use documentation links to explore services deeper
4. Spend extra time in Appendix 8.1 (Glossary) and 8.2 (Learning Resources)
5. Take detailed notes and build a home lab in the Azure free tier

Path C: Architect Using the Book as Reference

IF YOU'RE USING THIS book while working on live Azure projects:

1. Use the Table of Contents to locate specific architectural domains
2. Refer to diagrams, Bicep examples, and policy templates

3. Jump to best practices and trade-offs sections to support decision-making
4. Consult Chapter 8.3 and 8.4 for code snippets and reusable design patterns

---

Effective Study Practices

TO SUCCEED WITH THIS book, integrate it with active study strategies. Passive reading alone is insufficient. Adopt these approaches:

1. Use the Book Alongside a Sandbox Subscription

AZURE OFFERS A FREE trial account that includes:

- $200 credit for 30 days
- Limited usage of services like App Services, VMs, Storage, Functions

Create your own learning lab with:

- A dev subscription
- Management group hierarchy
- Log Analytics workspace
- Virtual networks with subnets and NSGs
- Storage account with lifecycle policies
- Web app with deployment slots

Use real deployments to match the architecture patterns discussed in the book.

2. Maintain a Personal Architecture Journal

WHILE READING, DOCUMENT your thoughts in an architecture decision log. For each topic, answer:

- What is the problem this service solves?
- What are alternatives and trade-offs?
- When would I recommend it in a real scenario?
- Are there compliance, performance, or cost implications?

Example entry:

Topic: Azure Site Recovery

Problem: Need DR for an on-premises SAP system

Trade-Offs:

- Pros: Fully managed, near-zero RPO

- Cons: Requires agent installation, cost increases with replication frequency

Alternative: Third-party DRaaS solution or cold standby with backups

Final Decision: Use ASR with Premium disks, replicate to secondary region

3. Practice Hands-On Labs

EACH CHAPTER INCLUDES optional labs or configurations to reinforce concepts. These are critical for retaining knowledge. Use the Azure CLI or Bicep over the portal to enforce repeatability.

Sample CLI sequence from Chapter 2 (RBAC and Identity):

az ad group create—display-name "NetworkAdmins"—mail-nickname "netadmins"

az role assignment create \

—assignee "NetworkAdmins" \

—role "Network Contributor" \

—scope "/subscriptions/<sub-id>/resourceGroups/network-rg"

Exam Alignment Markers

THE BOOK INCLUDES CALLOUTS like:

- **Exam Alert**: Direct indicators of high-frequency exam topics
- **Architect's Note**: Insightful perspectives drawn from enterprise experience
- **Decision Tree**: Diagrams to help evaluate between similar services
- **Cost Tip**: Highlights hidden pricing factors and optimization paths

These markers should not be skipped. Exam Alerts are usually based on Microsoft Learn guidance and known exam objectives.

Repetition and Retrieval: The Study Multiplier

TO EMBED KNOWLEDGE long-term:

- After reading each section, **summarize in your own words**
- Use spaced repetition—revisit notes every 3 days, then weekly

- Test recall: Write scenario-based questions and attempt to answer them cold
- Teach others: Explain a concept to a peer or record yourself articulating the idea

---

How to Approach Practice Questions (Chapter 7.2)

DO NOT TREAT THE QUESTIONS as trivia. Always:

- Read the question and scenario *twice*
- Eliminate obvious wrong choices first
- Identify trade-offs in each remaining answer
- Ask: "What is the Azure-native, scalable, and secure solution?"
- After answering, refer back to the book section that covers the topic

Example strategy question:

You're designing a multi-region web app with latency sensitivity. Which service should you use for routing and global failover?

A. Azure Load Balancer

B. Application Gateway

C. Azure Front Door

D. Azure Traffic Manager

Answer: **C. Azure Front Door**

Reason: Only Front Door provides global HTTP/HTTPS routing with SSL offloading, WAF integration, and latency-based failover.

Using the Appendices Strategically

Glossary (8.1)

QUICK REFERENCE FOR unfamiliar acronyms or terminology. Essential during exam cramming.

Resources (8.2)

CURATED SET OF MICROSOFT Learn paths, official documentation, whitepapers, and community blogs.

Sample Projects (8.3)

BLUEPRINTS AND GITHUB repos for deploying real-world solutions aligned to chapter themes.

API Reference (8.4)

CONVENIENT LOOKUPS for common REST and SDK calls for advanced readers or developers.

FAQs (8.5)

ANSWERS TO RECURRING questions about performance, security, limits, and design nuances.

Integrating With Other Resources

TO ROUND OUT YOUR PREPARATION:

- **Microsoft Learn**: Complete the AZ-305 modules

- **YouTube**: Watch short solution videos for visual retention
- **Pluralsight**: Use instructor-led courses for reinforcement
- **Whizlabs / MeasureUp**: Use practice exams to simulate test environment

---

Study Plan Template

8-WEEK EXAMPLE PLAN

Week	Focus Areas	Activities
1	Identity and Governance	Read Chapter 2, configure AAD, RBAC, Azure Policy
2	Monitoring and Cost Management	Read sections on Azure Monitor, Cost Alerts
3	Storage Design	Practice storage accounts, tiers, lifecycle rules
4	Resilience and Backup	Implement Backup Vaults, ASR, zone redundancy
5	Compute and Networking	Deploy VMs, App Services, Gateways, VNet peering
6	Application Design	Work with Functions, Logic Apps, API Management
7	Practice Questions	Take full mock exams, review errors
8	Final Review	Use glossaries, quick notes, and retry difficult topics

---

Summary

THIS BOOK IS YOUR ALL-in-one guide to passing AZ-305 and becoming a proficient Azure Solutions Architect. But its power lies in *how* you use it:

- Read with intention and curiosity
- Practice actively in Azure
- Take notes, summarize, and revisit often
- Use the book as a reference on the job

Approach your learning as a problem-solver, not a memorizer. Use each section to build a mental framework for Azure architecture. By the time you reach the final chapters, you won't just be exam-ready—you'll be job-ready.

Chapter 2: Designing Identity, Governance, and Monitoring Solutions

Architecting Azure Active Directory (Azure AD)

AZURE ACTIVE DIRECTORY (Azure AD) is the backbone of identity and access management in the Microsoft cloud ecosystem. For solution architects, understanding how to architect Azure AD is fundamental to designing secure, scalable, and compliant cloud solutions. Azure AD integrates identity, authentication, authorization, conditional access, and application access controls into a unified cloud-native platform.

This section explores the architectural foundations, core components, deployment patterns, and best practices of Azure AD from the perspective of an enterprise architect preparing for the AZ-305 exam and real-world implementations.

Core Concepts of Azure Active Directory

AZURE AD IS NOT A DIRECT replacement for traditional on-premises Active Directory (AD DS). It is a modern, cloud-based identity platform optimized for applications, cloud resources, and mobility. Understanding its core architectural elements is essential.

Tenants

A **tenant** represents a dedicated, isolated instance of Azure AD. Every Azure subscription is associated with one tenant. The tenant defines the identity boundary for all users, groups, and applications.

- Each tenant has a unique domain (e.g., contoso.onmicrosoft.com)
- You can add custom domains (e.g., contoso.com)
- A single tenant can manage multiple subscriptions

Directory Objects

KEY OBJECTS WITHIN Azure AD:

- **Users**: Cloud-only, synced from on-premises AD, or invited as B2B guests
- **Groups**: Used for access control—Security and Microsoft 365 groups
- **Devices**: Registered or joined devices used for Conditional Access
- **Service Principals**: Identity for applications or services
- **Managed Identities**: Secure identity for Azure services to authenticate without secrets

Identity Types

- **Cloud-only identity**: Created and managed entirely in Azure AD
- **Synchronized identity**: Synced from on-prem AD using Azure AD Connect
- **Federated identity**: Authentication delegated to external IdPs (e.g., ADFS, Okta)

Designing Identity Architecture with Azure AD

Multi-Tenant vs Single-Tenant Design

- **Single-Tenant**: Ideal for internal enterprise solutions with no external user access
- **Multi-Tenant**: Required when building SaaS apps intended for external organizations
- **B2B (Business-to-Business)**: External users are invited as guests to access resources
- **B2C (Business-to-Consumer)**: Public-facing apps with custom branding and support for social identities

Architectural Decision Matrix:

Scenario	Recommended Azure AD Model
Internal employees only	Single-tenant
External collaborators (e.g. partners)	Azure AD B2B
Consumer-facing app with user signup	Azure AD B2C
Multi-org SaaS platform	Multi-tenant + app registration

B2B Collaboration Architecture

AZURE AD B2B ALLOWS you to invite users from external tenants while enforcing your own access policies.

- External users retain their credentials from their home tenant
- Access is governed by your tenant's Conditional Access policies

- Ideal for partner portals, joint ventures, or supplier access

Steps:

1. Admin invites guest user via Azure portal or Graph API
2. User receives email and redeems invitation
3. Guest user can access assigned apps or groups

```
az ad user create—display-name "partner-user" \

—user-principal-name partner@externaldomain.com \

—invite-redirect-url https://mycompany.portal.com \

—force-change-password-next-login true
```

Identity Protection and Conditional Access

SECURITY IS CENTRAL to identity architecture. Azure AD provides advanced security controls:

Conditional Access

POLICIES THAT ENFORCE access control decisions based on:

- User identity
- Device compliance
- Location
- Application
- Risk level

Common Policies:

- Block legacy authentication
- Require MFA for admin accounts
- Require compliant devices for HR systems
- Block login from non-corporate IP ranges

```
{
"conditions": {
"signInRiskLevels": ["medium", "high"],
"clientAppTypes": ["browser", "mobileAppsAndDesktopClients"],
"locations": ["All trusted locations"]
},
"grantControls": {
"operator": "OR",
"builtInControls": ["mfa"]
}
}
```

Identity Protection

USES MACHINE LEARNING to detect suspicious login patterns and trigger policies:

- **Risky users**
- **Risky sign-ins**

- **User risk levels** (Low, Medium, High)

You can auto-remediate by enforcing password changes or requiring MFA.

Azure AD Roles and Privileged Access

AZURE AD IS BUILT AROUND **least privilege access**. To enforce this, the following components are crucial:

Role-Based Access Control (RBAC)

RBAC IN AZURE IS SCOPED and role-based:

- **Built-in roles**: Owner, Contributor, Reader, etc.
- **Custom roles**: Fine-grained permissions tailored to specific duties
- **Scope levels**: Management Group > Subscription > Resource Group > Resource

Use **Security Groups** or **AAD Groups** to assign access centrally.

Privileged Identity Management (PIM)

PIM ENABLES:

- Just-in-time access to Azure AD and Azure roles
- Time-bound role activation
- Approval workflows
- MFA and justification at activation time
- Audit logging

Use Case: Grant a developer temporary Contributor access for 2 hours to deploy a service.

Application Access and Single Sign-On (SSO)

AZURE AD ALLOWS CENTRAL authentication for internal and third-party applications:

- **SAML 2.0**, **OIDC**, and **OAuth 2.0** support
- Pre-integrated gallery with 3,000+ SaaS apps (e.g., Salesforce, ServiceNow, Workday)
- Ability to register custom applications for internal APIs or apps

Application Proxy

ALLOWS EXTERNAL ACCESS to internal apps without exposing them to the internet:

- Agents run inside the corporate network
- Azure AD provides authentication and Conditional Access
- No VPN required

Example Architecture:

- Internal HR portal published using Application Proxy
- Azure AD authenticates user with MFA
- Access logged and conditional on device compliance

Integrating On-Premises AD with Azure AD

FOR HYBRID IDENTITY, use **Azure AD Connect**:

- Synchronizes user, group, and device objects
- Supports password hash sync, pass-through auth, and federation
- Enables seamless SSO for on-prem users accessing cloud resources

Best Practices:

- Use Staging Mode for validation before switching to production
- Filter unnecessary OUs and attributes
- Monitor sync health with Azure AD Connect Health

For large orgs, consider **Azure AD Cloud Sync** for agent-based lightweight sync.

Design Patterns and Considerations

Pattern	When to Use	Key Benefit
Cloud-only identity	Greenfield apps, no on-prem AD	Simplicity, no sync complexity
Hybrid identity with SSO	Large enterprises with legacy systems	User convenience, no password change
B2B with Conditional Access	Partner portals and inter-company collaboration	Security without user migration
PIM with JIT Access	Administrative control with auditability	Least privilege and attack surface reduction
App Proxy for internal apps	Publish internal apps securely without VPN	Rapid enablement with cloud auth

Monitoring and Troubleshooting Identity

USE THE FOLLOWING TOOLS:

- **Azure AD Sign-in Logs**: Shows detailed logins, errors, MFA status, location
- **Audit Logs**: Tracks changes in directory roles, group memberships, app access
- **Workbooks and Alerts**: Build custom views for high-risk sign-ins
- **Graph Explorer or Microsoft Graph API**: Query and manipulate AAD data programmatically

GET https://graph.microsoft.com/v1.0/auditLogs/signIns?$filter=signInEventTypes eq 'interactive'&$top=50

Authorization: Bearer {token}

Set alerts for:

- Sign-ins from unfamiliar locations
- Role elevation events
- App consent changes

Summary

ARCHITECTING AZURE Active Directory involves more than configuring users and groups. It requires aligning identity strategy with business requirements, implementing strong security policies, and enabling seamless access across cloud, hybrid, and external collaboration scenarios.

Key takeaways for the AZ-305 exam and enterprise design:

- Choose identity models based on collaboration, access control, and app usage
- Secure identities with Conditional Access and Identity Protection
- Integrate hybrid identities using Azure AD Connect with best practices
- Use PIM and RBAC to enforce least privilege across the environment
- Centralize application access with SSO, App Proxy, and Graph APIs
- Monitor identity health with logs, alerts, and real-time analytics

In the next section, we will explore how to design granular access control strategies using Role-Based Access Control (RBAC) to enforce security and governance boundaries across subscriptions and resources.

Designing Role-Based Access Control (RBAC) Strategies

ROLE-BASED ACCESS CONTROL (RBAC) in Microsoft Azure is a foundational component for managing security and access at scale. It allows administrators and architects to control who has access to Azure resources, what they can do with those resources, and what areas they can access. For Azure Solutions Architects preparing for the AZ-305 exam or deploying secure environments in production, a deep understanding of RBAC design patterns, best practices, and governance strategies is essential.

This section covers the architecture of RBAC, its components, scoping and inheritance, role types, identity integration, least privilege enforcement, and real-world deployment scenarios. You will also explore how to architect RBAC policies for multi-subscription environments, automation strategies, and compliance controls.

Fundamentals of Azure RBAC

RBAC ENABLES **fine-grained access control** to Azure resources. It is built on three core principles:

1. **Security Principal** – Who: A user, group, service principal, or managed identity.
2. **Role Definition** – What: A collection of permissions (e.g., read, write, delete).
3. **Scope** – Where: The boundary over which the permissions apply.

An **RBAC assignment** is the binding of a principal to a role definition at a specific scope.

RBAC Assignment Formula:

Access = (Security Principal) + (Role Definition) + (Scope)

RBAC Scope and Hierarchy

SCOPES DEFINE THE BOUNDARIES of access and allow inheritance. Azure supports four hierarchical scopes:

- **Management Group** (top-level)
- **Subscription**
- **Resource Group**
- **Resource**

Assignments at a higher level flow downward. For example, assigning a role at the subscription level automatically applies to all resource groups and resources within that subscription.

Best Practice: Always assign access at the **lowest scope** necessary to follow the principle of least privilege.

Example CLI Assignment (Reader role at Resource Group level):

az role assignment create \

—assignee user@contoso.com \

—role Reader \

—resource-group dev-rg

Built-In Roles vs Custom Roles

AZURE OFFERS OVER 60 built-in roles, each with predefined permissions. Common ones include:

Role Name	Description
Owner	Full access, including RBAC management
Contributor	Full access except RBAC management
Reader	View-only access
Virtual Machine Contributor	Manage VMs but not network/ storage
Storage Blob Data Contributor	Read/write blobs only

Built-in roles cover most needs, but **custom roles** are essential for tailoring permissions precisely.

Creating Custom Roles

CUSTOM ROLES ARE JSON definitions that include actions, notActions, dataActions, and notDataActions.

Sample Custom Role JSON (Read-only access to compute):

```
{
"Name": "Compute Reader",
"IsCustom": true,
"Description": "Can view compute resources only",
"Actions": [
"Microsoft.Compute/*/read",
"Microsoft.Network/*/read",
"Microsoft.Storage/*/read"
],
"NotActions": [],
"AssignableScopes": ["/subscriptions/<sub-id>"]
}
```

Create using Azure CLI:

```
az role definition create—role-definition compute-reader.json
```

RBAC and Identity Types

RBAC SUPPORTS VARIOUS identity types:

- **Users**: Individuals with AAD accounts
- **Groups**: Security groups or Microsoft 365 groups
- **Service Principals**: App registrations (used for CI/CD and app access)
- **Managed Identities**: System-assigned or user-assigned identities tied to Azure resources

Managed Identity Example:

```
az webapp identity assign—name myapp—resource-group prod-rg

az role assignment create—assignee <principalId> \

—role "Storage Blob Data Reader" \

—scope "/subscriptions/<sub-id>/resourceGroups/prod-rg/providers/Microsoft.Storage/storageAccounts/mystorage"
```

This enables the app to access blobs securely without hardcoding secrets.

Least Privilege and Segregation of Duties

ARCHITECTS MUST ENFORCE **least privilege** by assigning users only the permissions they need, nothing more. In practice, this includes:

- **Using Reader instead of Contributor** when write access isn't needed
- **Splitting responsibilities** between dev, ops, and security
- **Auditing role assignments regularly**
- **Using PIM** for just-in-time elevation of privileged roles

Example Segregation:

Role	Group
Reader	Auditors
Contributor (non-RBAC)	Developers
User Access Administrator	Identity Administrators
Network Contributor	Network Team

Designing RBAC for Multi-Subscription Environments

ENTERPRISES OFTEN WORK with multiple subscriptions for isolation, billing, or compliance. Effective RBAC design in this scenario involves:

1. Using Management Groups

ORGANIZE SUBSCRIPTIONS under **management groups** by:

- Environment: Production, Dev, Test
- Business Unit: Finance, HR, Engineering
- Region: Europe, North America

Assign roles at the **management group level** where global policy consistency is required.

2. Role Assignment via Groups

USE **AAD security groups** to simplify access management. Assign roles to groups rather than individuals.

az ad group create—display-name "DB Admins"—mail-nickname "db-admins" az role assignment create—assignee "DB Admins" \

—role "SQL DB Contributor" \

—scope "/subscriptions/<sub-id>/resourceGroups/database-rg"

3. Subscription-Specific Contributor Roles

PREVENT CROSS-SUBSCRIPTION control unless explicitly required.

Data Plane vs Control Plane RBAC

AZURE RBAC PRIMARILY controls the **management (control) plane**: who can deploy, modify, or delete resources.

For **data plane** access (actual data), you must assign **data actions**.

Resource Type	Control Plane Example	Data Plane Example
Blob Storage	Create/Delete storage account	Read/Write blobs
Key Vault	Add/remove secrets	Get/List secrets (data actions)
SQL Database	Create server	SQL authentication (not RBAC)

To access data plane securely, use:

- **Storage Blob Data Reader**
- **Key Vault Secrets User**

Auditing and Monitoring Role Assignments

TRACK CHANGES AND MONITOR potential risks via:

- **Azure Activity Logs**: Tracks role assignment events
- **Azure Monitor Alerts**: Notify on elevated permissions or high-risk changes
- **Workbooks**: Visualize role assignment sprawl
- **Access Reviews**: Periodic reviews of role assignments in Azure AD

PIM Integration: Audit who activated roles, when, and why.

Automating RBAC with Infrastructure as Code (IaC)

USE BICEP OR ARM TEMPLATES to define role assignments declaratively.

Sample Bicep Snippet:

```
resource roleAssignment 'Microsoft.Authorization/roleAssignments@2020-04-01-preview' = {

name: guid(resourceGroup().id, 'myAppRole', principalId)

properties: {

roleDefinitionId:
subscriptionResourceId('Microsoft.Authorization/roleDefinitions', 'b24988ac-6180-42a0-ab88-20f7382dd24c') // Contributor

principalId: principalId

scope: resourceGroup().id

}

}
```

Use this approach in CI/CD pipelines to ensure consistency and security as code.

RBAC and Compliance Frameworks

ARCHITECTS ARE OFTEN responsible for ensuring RBAC aligns with:

- **ISO 27001**: Access control and least privilege
- **HIPAA**: Restrict PHI data access
- **SOC 2**: Auditability of access changes

Use **Azure Policy** and **Blueprints** to enforce RBAC-related constraints, such as:

- Only owners can assign roles
- Role changes require MFA
- All Contributor role assignments must be logged

Common RBAC Design Pitfalls

Pitfall	Description	Solution
Overuse of Owner Role	Too much access, risk of misconfiguration	Use Contributor + User Access Admin instead
Assigning at Subscription by Default	Broad scope that propagates too far	Scope access at Resource Group or resource level
No RBAC for service principals	Services running with excessive privilege	Assign specific roles, use Managed Identities
Inconsistent group usage	Individual assignments hard to manage	Always assign roles to AAD security groups
Lack of role cleanup	Users retain access after project ends	Use Access Reviews and expiration policies

Summary

DESIGNING AN EFFECTIVE RBAC strategy in Azure is crucial for enforcing security, maintaining compliance, and ensuring operational clarity across enterprise cloud environments. Key architectural takeaways:

- Always apply the **principle of least privilege**
- Use **groups and PIM** to simplify and secure access control
- Define **custom roles** when built-in roles do not meet specific needs
- Integrate **RBAC into infrastructure as code**
- Audit and review role assignments continuously

RBAC is not just a technical feature—it's a strategic governance tool. In the next section, we'll build upon these principles by implementing Azure Policy and Blueprints to enforce rules and streamline governance across large-scale environments.

Implementing Azure Policy and Blueprints

GOVERNANCE IS A FOUNDATIONAL responsibility of an Azure Solutions Architect. While Role-Based Access Control (RBAC) defines *who* can perform actions, **Azure Policy** and **Azure Blueprints** define *what* can be deployed and *how* those resources must be configured. These services enable organizations to ensure regulatory compliance, enforce organizational standards, and create repeatable, secure, and compliant environments.

This section provides in-depth guidance on designing and implementing Azure Policy and Blueprints. You'll explore their architecture, use cases, enforcement modes, auditing mechanisms, and integration into CI/CD and large-scale enterprise governance.

Azure Policy: Architecture and Purpose

AZURE POLICY IS A SERVICE that allows you to create, assign, and manage policy definitions that enforce rules on your Azure resources. Policies can allow, deny, audit, or append configurations during or after resource deployment.

Core Components

- **Policy Definition**: JSON document that defines the rule and its effect.

- **Initiative (Policy Set)**: A collection of policies grouped together.

- **Assignment**: Binding of a policy or initiative to a scope (management group, subscription, resource group, or resource).
- **Parameters**: Input values that make definitions reusable.

Common Effects:

- Deny: Blocks non-compliant resource creation or update
- Audit: Flags non-compliant resources but allows them
- Append: Adds properties to resource configurations
- DeployIfNotExists: Deploys a resource if it doesn't exist
- Modify: Alters properties of existing resources

Designing Effective Policy Definitions

A POLICY DEFINITION consists of two main parts:

1. **Conditions**: Evaluate the properties of a resource
2. **Effect**: Action taken when the condition is met

Example: Deny Public IP Address Creation

```
{
"properties": {
"displayName": "Deny Public IP",
"mode": "All",
"policyRule": {
"if": {
```

```
"field": "type",
"equals": "Microsoft.Network/publicIPAddresses"
},
"then": {
"effect": "deny"
}
}
}
}
```

This policy, when assigned, blocks the creation of Public IPs across the scoped resource hierarchy.

Best Practices

- USE AUDIT WHEN TESTING a new policy to observe its effect without blocking users.
- Add parameters to support dynamic input (e.g., allowed SKUs, locations).
- Use policy aliases (e.g., Microsoft.Compute/virtualMachines/sku.name) to reference fields.

Policy Assignment and Scoping

LIKE RBAC, AZURE POLICY supports hierarchical scoping:

- Management Group (global)

- Subscription
- Resource Group
- Individual Resource

Assignments at higher scopes cascade down, making it easier to enforce policies uniformly.

Example CLI Assignment:

az policy assignment create \

—name "denyPublicIP" \

—policy "/providers/Microsoft.Authorization/policyDefinitions/deny-public-ip" \

—scope "/subscriptions/xxxxxxxx-xxxx-xxxx-xxxx-xxxxxxxxxxxx"

Non-Compliance Reporting

AZURE POLICY AUTOMATICALLY evaluates and displays compliance results:

- **Compliant:** Resource meets the policy conditions.
- **Non-Compliant:** Resource violates the policy rules.

You can view these results via Azure Portal, REST API, or CLI.

az policy state list—query "[?complianceState=='NonCompliant']"

Common Use Cases for Azure Policy

Use Case	Example Policy
Enforce resource location	Only deploy in UK South or West Europe
Control VM SKU types	Restrict to Standard_B2s, Standard_D2s_v3
Tag enforcement	Require CostCenter and Environment tags
Encryption enforcement	Audit if disks are not encrypted with CMK
Limit public exposure	Deny public IPs, require Private Endpoints
Cost management	Restrict Premium SKUs for Dev/Test environments

SAMPLE POLICY: ENFORCE Tag and Value

```
{
"properties": {
"displayName": "Enforce CostCenter Tag",
"parameters": {
"tagName": {
"type": "String",
"defaultValue": "CostCenter"
},
"tagValue": {
"type": "String",
"defaultValue": "Finance"
```

```
}
},
"policyRule": {
"if": {
"not": {
"field": "[concat('tags[', parameters('tagName'), ']')]",
"equals": "[parameters('tagValue')]"
}
},
"then": {
"effect": "deny"
}
}
}
}
```

Initiatives: Scaling with Policy Sets

AN **Initiative** is a collection of policies grouped under one logical assignment. This allows centralized management and reporting for compliance across multiple related policies.

Use Cases:

- Apply a compliance standard like ISO 27001 or NIST

• Enforce all tagging, networking, and identity rules in one initiative

• Assign company-wide governance rules at the management group level

Example CLI:

az policy set-definition create \

—name "org-compliance" \

—definitions '[{"policyDefinitionId": "/providers/.../policyDefinitions/deny-public-ip"}]' \

—display-name "Organizational Compliance"

DeployIfNotExists and Modify

THESE EFFECTS ARE ADVANCED enforcement tools:

• **DeployIfNotExists (DINE)**: If a required resource is missing, Azure Policy can deploy it using a template (e.g., ensure diagnostic settings exist).

• **Modify**: Update or insert missing properties (e.g., force HTTPS on App Services).

Use Case: Enforce diagnostics on all Key Vaults

• Create a policy with a DeployIfNotExists effect

• Reference an ARM template that configures diagnostic settings

• Assign it to a scope such as subscription or management group

Azure Blueprints: Environment-as-Code

WHILE AZURE POLICY enforces rules, **Azure Blueprints** define **complete environments** including:

- Resource groups
- RBAC assignments
- Policy assignments
- ARM templates

Blueprints are designed for **governance at scale**—ideal for regulated industries or centralized IT departments.

Key Components

- **Blueprint Definition**: The template for the environment
- **Artifacts**: Components included (policies, roles, templates)
- **Assignment**: Applying the blueprint to a specific subscription

Use Cases:

- Standardize subscription provisioning for new teams
- Ensure every subscription has backup policies, logging, and network rules
- Delegate controlled environments to business units

Sample Artifacts in a Blueprint:

- Audit policy for encryption
- Tag policy enforcement

- Role assignment for security team
- Resource group with ARM-deployed NSG

Blueprint Lifecycle

1. **Create Definition**: Define artifacts in Blueprint portal or via ARM
2. **Publish Blueprint**: Set version for assignment
3. **Assign Blueprint**: Apply to one or more subscriptions
4. **Lock Resources**: Optionally prevent resource modification or deletion

BLUEPRINT LOCKING MODES:

- **Don't Lock**: Resources are modifiable
- **Read Only**: Prevents changes
- **Do Not Delete**: Resources cannot be deleted

Policy vs Blueprint: When to Use Each

Feature	Azure Policy	Azure Blueprints
Purpose	Enforce compliance	Deploy standardized environments
Includes Resource Deployments	Only with DINE/Modify	Full ARM template and resource group support
RBAC Assignment	No	Yes
Policy Assignment	Yes	Yes
Locking Support	No	Yes
Versioning	No	Yes

BEST PRACTICE: Use **Policy** for continuous compliance enforcement and **Blueprints** for initial subscription setup and governance bootstrapping.

Integration into DevOps and CI/CD

FOR LARGE ORGANIZATIONS, governance must be codified and automated.

Policy as Code:

- Store policy JSON files in Git
- Use pipelines (GitHub Actions, Azure DevOps) to deploy definitions and assignments

Blueprint as Code:

- Blueprints can be exported as ARM templates
- Use Azure DevOps release pipelines for version control

Pipeline Sample:

```
- task: AzureCLI@2

inputs:

azureSubscription: 'Prod Connection'

scriptType: 'bash'

scriptLocation: 'inlineScript'

inlineScript: |

az policy assignment create—name "enforce-tags" \
```

—policy "enforce-tags.json" \

—scope "/subscriptions/xxxx..."

This ensures policy governance is part of the application lifecycle.

Monitoring Policy Compliance

USE **Azure Policy Compliance** dashboards:

- Visual compliance per initiative or policy
- Export reports for audit use
- Drill-down to non-compliant resources

Automation:

- Set alerts for high non-compliance percentage
- Trigger remediation actions
- Use Azure Resource Graph queries to identify policy drift

Example KQL (Log Analytics):

```
PolicyResources
| where ComplianceState == "NonCompliant"
| summarize count() by PolicyDefinitionName
```

Summary

AZURE POLICY AND BLUEPRINTS are essential tools for designing secure, compliant, and standardized Azure environments. They allow architects to shift governance left—embedding it into infrastructure provisioning and application deployment processes.

Key Practices:

- Use **Azure Policy** to enforce guardrails continuously
- Deploy **Initiatives** to manage policies at scale
- Leverage **DeployIfNotExists** for auto-remediation
- Use **Blueprints** for initial subscription or environment bootstrapping
- Automate deployment of policies and assignments using CI/CD
- Monitor and audit compliance with dashboards, alerts, and resource graph queries

By designing and enforcing governance at scale, architects ensure not only technical integrity but organizational trust in the cloud. In the next section, we'll explore how to centralize monitoring using Azure Monitor, Log Analytics, and Application Insights to create an operational feedback loop across the entire environment.

Centralizing Monitoring with Azure Monitor and Log Analytics

EFFECTIVE MONITORING is a cornerstone of resilient and scalable cloud architecture. In Azure, monitoring is not a single tool, but a **comprehensive observability framework** built around Azure Monitor, Log Analytics, Application Insights, and related services. These components enable architects to collect telemetry, detect anomalies, diagnose incidents, ensure compliance, and continuously improve operational performance.

This section explains how to architect centralized monitoring using Azure-native tools. It explores architectural patterns, data sources, integration strategies, automation, and best practices for monitoring hybrid and distributed systems—aligned with the demands of the AZ-305 certification and real-world governance.

Overview of Azure Monitor

AZURE MONITOR IS THE central service for collecting, analyzing, and acting on telemetry from Azure resources, applications, and operating systems.

Core Capabilities

- **Metrics**: Numerical time-series data for performance (CPU %, memory, request rate)
- **Logs**: Structured/unstructured data from events, diagnostics, and traces
- **Alerts**: Rules based on metrics/log queries to notify or auto-remediate
- **Dashboards & Workbooks**: Visualizations for stakeholders
- **Insights**: Pre-built monitoring experiences for specific services (e.g., VM Insights)

Azure Monitor acts as the hub that connects signals from VMs, containers, PaaS services, and third-party integrations.

Architecture of a Centralized Monitoring Solution

A SCALABLE MONITORING solution includes:

1. **Data Collection**
    - Agents or built-in diagnostics

   ○ Metrics, logs, traces, and custom telemetry

2. **Ingestion and Storage**
   ○ Log Analytics Workspace (for logs)
   ○ Azure Monitor Metrics (for metrics)

3. **Visualization**
   ○ Workbooks, Dashboards, Grafana, Power BI

4. **Detection**
   ○ Metric and log-based alerts
   ○ Smart detection in Application Insights

5. **Response**
   ○ Automated actions (Logic Apps, Functions)
   ○ Notifications (email, SMS, ITSM)

6. **Analysis and Continuous Improvement**
   ○ Kusto Query Language (KQL)
   ○ Azure Monitor Logs and Analytics

Log Analytics Workspace

A **Log Analytics Workspace** is the central repository for logs collected by Azure Monitor. Every Azure resource that supports diagnostic logging can send data here.

Workspace Design Considerations:

- **Centralized vs Per-subscription**:
  - Centralized workspace simplifies cross-resource analysis
  - Per-subscription workspaces improve isolation but increase complexity
- **Data retention**: Configurable up to 2 years
- **Access control**: Use RBAC and table-level permissions

Create via CLI:

```
az monitor log-analytics workspace create \
—resource-group ops-rg \
—workspace-name org-monitoring \
—location westeurope
```

Connecting Azure Resources to Log Analytics

MANY AZURE SERVICES natively support diagnostic settings. These allow logs and metrics to be forwarded to:

- Log Analytics Workspace
- Event Hub
- Storage Account

Example: Enable diagnostics for a storage account

```
az monitor diagnostic-settings create \
```

—name "diag-logs" \

—resource "/subscriptions/xxx/resourceGroups/ops-rg/providers/Microsoft.Storage/storageAccounts/mystorage" \

—workspace "/subscriptions/xxx/resourceGroups/ops-rg/providers/Microsoft.OperationalInsights/workspaces/org-monitoring" \

—logs '[{"category": "StorageRead", "enabled": true}]'

Resources that support diagnostics include:

- Azure VMs
- App Services
- Azure SQL
- Key Vault
- Network Security Groups
- Load Balancers
- API Management

Kusto Query Language (KQL)

KQL IS THE QUERY LANGUAGE used to retrieve and analyze data from Log Analytics. Mastery of KQL is critical for designing effective monitoring solutions.

Example Queries:

1. **Count failed logins across resources**

SigninLogs

| where ResultType != 0

| summarize count() by bin(TimeGenerated, 1h)

1. **Find all VMs with CPU usage > 80%**

Perf

| where CounterName == "% Processor Time"

| summarize AvgCPU = avg(CounterValue) by bin(TimeGenerated, 5m), Computer

| where AvgCPU > 80

1. **List top 10 IP addresses hitting App Gateway**

AzureDiagnostics

| where ResourceType == "APPLICATIONGATEWAYS"

| summarize Requests = count() by clientIP_s

| top 10 by Requests

These queries can power workbooks, alerts, and export automation.

Alerting Strategy

ALERTS ENABLE PROACTIVE detection of issues. They can be metric-based or log-based.

Metric Alerts

- TRIGGERED WHEN A threshold is breached
- Fast response time (near real-time)

- Use for CPU, memory, latency, etc.

Example: VM CPU > 90% for 10 minutes

```
az monitor metrics alert create \
—name "highCPU" \
—resource "/subscriptions/xxx/resourceGroups/rg1/providers/Microsoft.Compute/virtualMachines/vm1" \
—condition "avg Percentage CPU > 90" \
—window-size 10m \
—evaluation-frequency 1m
```

Log Alerts

- TRIGGERED BY QUERY results in Log Analytics
- Useful for complex conditions (e.g., error rate spikes, anomaly detection)

Example: HTTP 500 errors from App Service

```
AppRequests
| where ResultCode == 500
| summarize Count = count() by bin(TimeGenerated, 5m)
```

Application Insights

APPLICATION INSIGHTS is an extension of Azure Monitor that provides deep observability for applications.

Key Features:

- SERVER-SIDE AND client-side telemetry
- Automatic dependency tracking (HTTP calls, databases)
- Distributed tracing with correlation IDs
- Smart detection of anomalies
- Custom events and metrics

Languages supported:

- .NET, Java, Node.js, Python, Go, PHP

Setup Example (for Node.js):

```
npm install applicationinsights

const appInsights = require("applicationinsights");

appInsights.setup("INSTRUMENTATION_KEY").start();
```

Once enabled, you gain visibility into:

- Request rates and response times
- Failures by exception type
- Slow dependencies
- User sessions and geography

Workbooks and Dashboards

WORKBOOKS allow the creation of rich, interactive reports and dashboards using KQL queries, metrics, and visuals. They are ideal for:

- Executive reports (SLAs, uptime)
- Security dashboards (failed logins, policy violations)
- Cost visibility (metrics vs usage)

Dashboards are simpler, faster-loading alternatives for frequent use.

Use Case Examples:

- Combine App Insights and Key Vault logs to track unauthorized access
- Overlay VM metrics with storage I/O to correlate performance
- Monitor AKS cluster health with container metrics and pod logs

---

Integrating with Azure Arc and Hybrid Environments

AZURE MONITOR AND LOG Analytics support **Azure Arc** to extend monitoring to:

- On-premises servers
- Multi-cloud resources (AWS EC2, GCP VMs)
- Kubernetes clusters (via Azure Monitor for containers)

Use Case:

- Connect non-Azure servers to central monitoring

- Apply log alerts and policy compliance uniformly

Automating Monitoring Setup

INFRASTRUCTURE AS CODE (IaC) and policy enforcement should include monitoring setup. Use:

- **ARM/Bicep** for workspace, diagnostic settings, alert rules
- **Azure Policy** to enforce diagnostics on resource creation
- **Blueprints** to embed monitoring in subscription provisioning

Sample Bicep Snippet:

```
resource diag 'Microsoft.Insights/diagnosticSettings@2021-05-01-preview' = {
name: 'enableDiag'
scope: storageAccount
properties: {
workspaceId: logAnalyticsWorkspace.id
logs: [
{
category: 'StorageRead'
enabled: true
}
]
}
```

```
}
```

Cost Considerations

MONITORING GENERATES data—understanding costs is vital:

- **Data ingestion**: Charged per GB
- **Retention**: Free for 31 days, then charge per GB/month
- **Queries**: Free, but exporting or frequent queries via API can increase costs

Optimization Tips:

- Filter unnecessary logs at source
- Use sampling in Application Insights
- Separate Dev/Test workspaces with short retention

Summary

AZURE MONITOR AND LOG Analytics form the backbone of an intelligent, scalable, and secure observability platform. Designing centralized monitoring ensures that all telemetry is collected, analyzed, and actioned in real-time, providing unmatched visibility into the health, performance, and compliance of your Azure environment.

Architectural Best Practices:

- Use a **centralized Log Analytics Workspace** for enterprise monitoring
- Enable diagnostics on all mission-critical resources

- Create **custom KQL dashboards** tailored to different audiences
- Automate setup via **IaC and Azure Policy**
- Monitor hybrid resources using **Azure Arc**
- Establish **alerting thresholds and smart detection** for early warnings
- Balance **retention and data ingestion** for cost-effective operations

In the next section, we will examine governance frameworks and cost management tools that help enforce enterprise standards while optimizing spending across large Azure environments.

Governance Best Practices and Cost Management Tools

EFFECTIVE GOVERNANCE in Azure ensures that cloud environments remain secure, compliant, manageable, and cost-optimized at scale. Governance is not a singular action, but a **strategic framework** encompassing people, policies, processes, and tools. Azure provides built-in capabilities such as Management Groups, Policies, Blueprints, Cost Management, Tags, Budgets, and more to help organizations establish and enforce governance across multiple teams, workloads, and environments.

This section explores enterprise-scale governance strategies, management hierarchy design, policy enforcement models, tagging and resource organization, cost visibility and budgeting tools, and automation techniques. These principles are essential both for real-world solution architects and for success in the AZ-305 exam.

Governance and the Azure Enterprise Scaffold

THE **Enterprise-Scale Landing Zone model** developed by Microsoft defines a standard scaffold for cloud governance. It helps organizations set up guardrails and control planes before workloads are deployed.

Core Pillars of Governance:

1. **Management Group Hierarchy**
2. **Resource Organization and Tagging**
3. **Role-Based Access Control (RBAC)**
4. **Policy and Blueprint Enforcement**
5. **Cost Management and Budgets**
6. **Monitoring and Operational Consistency**
7. **Automation and Repeatability**

THESE PILLARS FORM the basis of a **Cloud Operating Model** and ensure consistency across development, staging, and production environments.

Designing a Management Group Hierarchy

AZURE **Management Groups** allow you to organize subscriptions and apply controls (RBAC, Policy, Blueprints) across them hierarchically.

Example Hierarchy:

TENANT ROOT GROUP

├── Platform

│ ├── Identity

```
│ └── Connectivity
├── Management
│ ├── Monitoring
│ └── Security
├── Landing Zones
│ ├── Dev
│ ├── Test
│ └── Prod
```

Best Practices:

- Use the Tenant Root Group to apply global policies like allowed locations.
- Group subscriptions by **environment**, **business unit**, or **compliance zone**.
- Apply **RBAC and Policies at the highest scope** where appropriate to reduce duplication.

Create via CLI:

az account management-group create—name "LandingZones"—display-name "Landing Zones"

Resource Organization and Naming Standards

A CONSISTENT AND ENFORCEABLE **resource naming convention** enables:

- Easy identification and filtering

- Simplified automation
- Accurate cost tracking
- Improved auditability

Example Naming Convention:

Resource Type	Pattern	Example
Resource Group	<project>-<env>-rg	finance-prod-rg
Storage Account	<app><env>stg	invoicerdevstg
Key Vault	kv-<app>-<region>	kv-api-uksouth
Virtual Network	vnet-<dept>-<env>	vnet-it-prod

Azure Resource Graph

QUERY AND VISUALIZE resource metadata using Resource Graph:

```
Resources

| where type =~ 'microsoft.compute/virtualmachines'

| project name, location, tags
```

Tagging Strategy and Enforcement

TAGS are metadata key-value pairs that help organize resources. Tags are critical for:

- Cost allocation by team, environment, or application
- Compliance tracking
- Lifecycle management

Tag Categories:

Tag Key	Purpose
CostCenter	Chargeback/billing
Environment	Dev, Test, Staging, Prod
Owner	Responsible team or person
Retention	Archival policy
Confidentiality	Data classification (Public/Internal/Secret)

Tagging Policy Example:

```
{
"policyRule": {
"if": {
"field": "[concat('tags[', parameters('tagName'), ']')]",
"exists": "false"
},
"then": {
"effect": "deny"
}
},
"parameters": {
"tagName": {
"type": "String",
"defaultValue": "CostCenter"
}
```

}

}

Use **Azure Policy** to enforce tags during resource creation and remediation.

Cost Management Overview

AZURE COST MANAGEMENT + Billing provides visibility into resource usage, spending, and trends. It supports:

- Daily cost breakdown
- Forecasting
- Resource-level chargeback
- Budget enforcement
- Advisor recommendations for cost savings

Key Interfaces:

- Azure Portal (Cost Analysis)
- REST APIs
- Power BI connectors
- Azure CLI (for scripts and automation)

Budgets and Alerts

BUDGETS allow you to set thresholds for spending and receive alerts proactively. Budgets are scoped at the subscription, resource group, or management group level.

Example Budget Setup (CLI):

az consumption budget create \

—amount 5000 \

—category cost \

—name "monthly-prod-budget" \

—start-date 2025-01-01 \

—end-date 2026-01-01 \

—time-grain monthly \

—subscription-id xxxxxxxx-xxxx-xxxx-xxxx-xxxxxxxxxxxx \

—notifications actualGt80 \

enabled=true \

operator=GreaterThan \

threshold=80 \

contactEmails=user1@contoso.com user2@contoso.com

Best Practices:

- Set **different thresholds** (80%, 90%, 100%) to trigger staged responses.
- Use **automated actions** like scaling down non-critical services when nearing limits.
- Align budgets with **tags** to enforce per-team cost accountability.

Azure Advisor Recommendations

AZURE ADVISOR PROVIDES real-time, actionable guidance for:

- **Cost optimization**: Right-sizing, reserved instances
- **High availability**: Redundancy, SLAs
- **Security**: Defender recommendations
- **Operational excellence**: Monitoring and governance

Export Advisor findings to Power BI or integrate into CI/CD for validation gates.

Advisor CLI Example:

```
az advisor recommendation list—category Cost
```

Cost Allocation and Chargeback Models

TO ASSIGN CLOUD SPEND to business units, use:

- **Management Groups**: For high-level division
- **Tags**: For granular filtering (e.g., per application)
- **Resource Groups**: Grouped resources per team or service

Power BI or **Excel exports** can visualize:

- Spend per cost center
- Trends over time
- Budget variance

Use Azure Cost Management's **export feature** to generate daily reports in Storage for external processing.

Automation and Governance as Code

USE INFRASTRUCTURE as Code to define governance controls consistently:

- **ARM templates** or **Bicep** to deploy policies, initiatives, and assignments
- **Terraform** modules for managing cost and policy resources
- **Blueprints** to combine RBAC, policies, and deployments

Sample Bicep to Assign Policy and Tag

```
resource tagPolicy 'Microsoft.Authorization/policyAssignments@2020-09-01' = {

name: 'requireTags'

scope: resourceGroup().id

properties: {

policyDefinitionId: policyDefinition.id

parameters: {

tagName: { value: 'Environment' }

}

}

}
```

Automate via **Azure DevOps** or **GitHub Actions** to embed governance into CI/CD.

Compliance and Auditing

AZURE SUPPORTS BUILT-in compliance frameworks:

- ISO 27001
- HIPAA
- NIST SP 800-53
- CIS Benchmarks

Use **Policy Initiatives** and **Defender for Cloud** to continuously validate compliance.

Compliance Reporting Tools:

- **Azure Policy Compliance** (initiative-based scoring)
- **Microsoft Purview** (data classification and risk reporting)
- **Defender for Cloud Regulatory Compliance Dashboard**

Sample KQL for Audit Events:

```
AuditLogs
| where ActivityDisplayName == "Add member to role"
| project TimeGenerated, InitiatedBy, TargetResources
```

Governance Maturity Levels

Level	Description	Characteristics
1	Ad-hoc Governance	Inconsistent tagging, no policy enforcement
2	Reactive Governance	Policies exist but not monitored
3	Proactive Governance	Automated tagging, policy compliance alerts
4	Embedded Governance in CI/CD	Governance deployed via IaC and pipelines
5	Autonomous Governance	AI-driven cost optimization, self-healing guardrails

AIM FOR LEVELS 4–5 for robust, self-sustaining governance models.

Summary

EFFECTIVE GOVERNANCE in Azure requires an architectural approach that integrates people, processes, and tools. By leveraging Azure's built-in governance and cost management features, organizations can control cloud sprawl, optimize cost, maintain security and compliance, and ensure operational excellence.

Key Practices for Architects:

- Build a management group structure aligned with business boundaries
- Enforce tags using policies to track cost and compliance
- Use Azure Policy and Blueprints for guardrails and automation
- Set budgets and alerts to prevent overspend

- Visualize cost and compliance via dashboards and reports
- Automate governance using infrastructure as code and CI/CD
- Continuously monitor compliance posture using Azure-native tools

In the next chapter, we will shift our focus to **data storage architectures**, where you'll learn how to choose the right Azure storage services and design secure, performant, and scalable data strategies.

Chapter 3: Designing Data Storage Solutions

Selecting the Right Storage Account Types

CHOOSING THE APPROPRIATE storage account type in Azure is a foundational architectural decision that significantly affects cost, performance, scalability, availability, and security. Azure offers a rich set of storage options, each designed for different scenarios such as general-purpose workloads, unstructured data, archival, big data analytics, and high-performance computing.

In this section, we will explore the architecture, characteristics, and selection criteria for the different types of storage accounts available in Azure. We'll analyze trade-offs, design patterns, performance tiers, and real-world scenarios to help you confidently architect data storage solutions aligned with the AZ-305 certification and enterprise needs.

Overview of Azure Storage Account Types

AT A HIGH LEVEL, AZURE provides two broad categories of storage accounts:

1. **General-purpose v2 (GPv2)** — The default and most flexible account type
2. **Specialized storage accounts** — Optimized for specific workloads

Within these categories, storage accounts can be configured with different redundancy, performance, and access tiers. Selecting the correct combination is critical to meeting non-functional requirements (NFRs) such as durability, latency, and cost.

General-purpose v2 (GPv2)

GPV2 is the most commonly used storage account type and supports:

- **Blob Storage** (Block blobs, Append blobs, Page blobs)
- **File Shares** (SMB)
- **Queues** (Message queuing)
- **Tables** (NoSQL key-value store)
- **Disks** (when used with managed disks)

Key Features:

- SUPPORTS HOT, COOL, and Archive tiers for Blob
- Can host static websites using Blob Storage
- Fully compatible with Azure Data Lake Storage Gen2 (when enabled)
- Integration with Azure Monitor, diagnostics, and logging
- RBAC and role-based storage access
- Virtual Network and firewall support

Use Cases:

- Web and mobile app data
- Backup and disaster recovery

- Event-driven architectures
- File sharing across VMs

Premium Performance Tiers

FOR LATENCY-SENSITIVE applications, **Premium storage** is available in two flavors:

Premium Block Blob

- USES SSD-BACKED storage
- Low-latency, high-throughput blob access
- Ideal for analytics, media rendering, and telemetry ingestion

Premium File Storage

- ENTERPRISE-GRADE SMB file shares on SSDs
- Suitable for lift-and-shift applications needing high IOPS

Premium Page Blobs (Disks)

- USED FOR AZURE MANAGED Disks
- Required for high-performance VMs (e.g., M-series)

Blob Storage Accounts (Legacy)

BLOB STORAGE ACCOUNTS are a legacy type (pre-GPv2) that only support blob workloads. They allow tiering per blob and are limited in features compared to GPv2.

Recommendation: Use GPv2 unless you have a legacy application dependency.

Azure Data Lake Storage Gen2

ADLS GEN2 is built on top of Blob Storage and adds hierarchical namespace and POSIX-compliant access control.

Key Features:

- OPTIMIZED FOR BIG data analytics
- Supports Hadoop Distributed File System (HDFS)
- Efficient directory operations (move, rename, list)
- Fine-grained access control using Azure RBAC and ACLs

Use Cases:

- Data lakes for analytics
- Machine learning feature stores
- Centralized storage for data pipelines

Enable during creation:

az storage account create \

—name datalakeaccount \

—resource-group rg-data \

—location uksouth \

—sku Standard_LRS \

—kind StorageV2 \

—hierarchical-namespace true

Storage Redundancy Options

REDUNDANCY DETERMINES how data is replicated across data centers or regions to protect against data loss.

Redundancy Option	Description	Use Case
LRS (Locally Redundant Storage)	3 copies in a single datacenter	Non-critical data with limited durability needs
ZRS (Zone-Redundant Storage)	3 copies across availability zones	High availability within region (VM disks, web apps)
GRS (Geo-Redundant Storage)	LRS + async copy to paired region	Business continuity with inter-region failover
RA-GRS (Read-Access GRS)	GRS with read access to secondary	Reporting or analytics on replicated data
GZRS / RA-GZRS	Zone + geo redundancy	Premium resiliency for mission-critical systems

Decision Factors:

- LRS: Cheapest, but single point of failure
- ZRS: Resilient within region; recommended for production apps
- GRS: Adds regional redundancy for DR but incurs higher latency and cost

- RA-GRS: Adds read access to secondary, ideal for BI workloads

Access Tiers for Blob Storage

AZURE BLOB STORAGE supports three access tiers to balance cost and performance:

Tier	Description	Use Case
Hot	Frequent access, lowest latency	Active apps, media content, CDN origin
Cool	Infrequent access, lower storage cost	Backup data, DR snapshots
Archive	Rare access, low storage, high retrieval cost	Regulatory archives, raw telemetry

Blobs can be moved between tiers manually or via lifecycle management policies.

Lifecycle Management Policy Example:

```
{
"rules": [
{
"name": "archive-old-logs",
"enabled": true,
"type": "Lifecycle",
"definition": {
"filters": {
"blobTypes": ["blockBlob"],
```

```
"prefixMatch": ["log/"]
},
"actions": {
"baseBlob": {
"tierToCool": {
"daysAfterModificationGreaterThan": 30
},
"tierToArchive": {
"daysAfterModificationGreaterThan": 90
}
}
}
}
}
]
}
```

Selecting the Right Storage Type: Decision Matrix

Requirement	Recommended Storage Type
General app storage (web/ mobile)	GPv2 (Blob/File/Table)
File share with SMB for lift-and-shift	Azure File Storage (Standard or Premium)
Machine learning training data	ADLS Gen2 with hierarchical namespace
High IOPS database backup	Premium Page Blob (managed disks)
Long-term archival of logs	Blob Storage Archive tier
Streaming telemetry ingestion	Premium Block Blob
Structured NoSQL key-value storage	Table Storage
Event queue for async processing	Azure Queue Storage

Storage Account Configuration Considerations

Network Access Control

- USE **Private Endpoints** for secure VNet integration
- Restrict public access with firewall rules
- Enable **Storage Firewall** to whitelist IP ranges

```
az storage account update \
—name mystorage \
—default-action Deny \
```

—bypass AzureServices

Security Features

- ENABLE **Soft Delete** for blobs, file shares, and containers
- Use **Azure AD RBAC** for identity-based access
- Encrypt data at rest using:
    - Microsoft-managed keys (default)
    - Customer-managed keys (CMK) via Key Vault
    - Double encryption for highly sensitive workloads

Monitoring and Logging

- ENABLE **Diagnostic Settings** to route logs to Log Analytics
- Use **Storage Metrics** for request counts, latency, and availability
- Set up alerts for throttling or unauthorized access

Multi-region and Multi-account Strategy

FOR GLOBAL WORKLOADS, consider:

- Deploying **multiple storage accounts per region** for performance scaling and compliance
- Using **Azure CDN** or **Front Door** to distribute data access
- Implementing **Geo-zone-redundant Storage** for mission-critical, global applications

- Architecting for **eventual consistency** across data replicas

---

Data Management and Automation

USE TOOLS LIKE:

- **AzCopy**: High-performance data transfer tool
- **Azure Data Factory**: ETL/ELT pipelines for structured and unstructured data
- **Azure CLI or Bicep** for repeatable deployments

Example: Upload with AzCopy

```
azcopy copy 'C:\logs' 'https://<account>.blob.core.windows.net/logs?<SAS>'—recursive
```

Summary

SELECTING THE CORRECT Azure storage account type is a foundational architectural decision that impacts every dimension of your cloud solution. You must balance cost, performance, redundancy, accessibility, and integration needs.

Architectural Best Practices:

- Default to **GPv2** unless a specialized workload requires otherwise
- Use **ADLS Gen2** for analytic workloads and Hadoop integration
- Choose **Premium tiers** only when low-latency or high-IOPS are needed
- Set **Blob tiers and lifecycle policies** to reduce storage costs
- Enable **diagnostics and monitoring** early to ensure visibility

- Use **Private Endpoints and CMKs** for secure and compliant access
- Design **multi-account and multi-region architectures** for resilience

In the next section, we will dive into designing data access patterns and redundancy models that ensure availability, consistency, and performance across varying application workloads.

Designing Data Access and Redundancy Models

DATA ACCESS AND REDUNDANCY are critical elements in architecting reliable, scalable, and secure cloud-native applications. Azure offers a wide variety of storage services and configurations, each tailored to different patterns of access, durability requirements, performance tiers, and availability models. As a Solutions Architect, it is your responsibility to understand how to design for optimal data accessibility, ensure availability through redundancy, and align storage strategies with business continuity and compliance requirements.

In this section, we'll explore core access models, redundancy strategies, consistency models, read/write architecture patterns, access optimization techniques, and Azure-native features that support enterprise-grade data design.

Understanding Data Access Patterns

THE FIRST STEP IN DESIGNING a robust data architecture is analyzing *how* data will be accessed. This includes frequency, latency sensitivity, throughput, and geographic distribution.

Common Access Patterns:

Pattern	Description	Example
Hot access	Frequent, low-latency reads/ writes	Application config, active user data
Cool/ infrequent access	Accessed weekly or monthly	Archived invoices, logs
Sequential write, rare read	Append-only or telemetry ingestion	Logging, audit trails
Random read/ write	Unpredictable access across objects	User-uploaded files, analytics data
Streaming	Continuous read/write in small chunks	Media, telemetry, event ingestion
Batch read/ write	Periodic full read/write workloads	Reporting, data sync jobs
Geo-distributed read	Read-heavy applications across multiple regions	Global CDN, public websites

DESIGNING FOR THE CORRECT access pattern ensures reduced costs, improved performance, and better user experience.

Access Tiers and Lifecycle Design

AZURE BLOB STORAGE supports three **access tiers**: Hot, Cool, and Archive. Each is optimized for different frequency-of-access and cost trade-offs.

Tier	Optimized For	Use Case	Retrieval Time
Hot	Frequent access	App data, active logs	Instant
Cool	Infrequent access	Backups, seasonal data	Instant
Archive	Rare access	Compliance data, legal archives	Hours

Lifecycle Policies automatically move blobs between tiers based on age or last modified date:

```
{
"rules": [
{
"enabled": true,
"name": "archive-after-90",
"definition": {
"actions": {
"baseBlob": {
"tierToCool": {
"daysAfterModificationGreaterThan": 30
},
"tierToArchive": {
"daysAfterModificationGreaterThan": 90
}
```

```
}
},
"filters": {
"blobTypes": [ "blockBlob" ],
"prefixMatch": [ "logs/" ]
}
}
}
]
}
```

Redundancy Models in Azure Storage

REDUNDANCY IS ESSENTIAL to ensuring data availability and durability. Azure offers multiple replication models that protect against hardware failure, zone failure, and regional disaster.

Azure Storage Replication Options

Replication Type	Copies	Scope	Use Case
LRS	3	Single datacenter	Dev/test workloads
ZRS	3	Across availability zones	SLA-bound apps within one region
GRS	6	Primary + paired region	Regulatory backup, DR readiness
RA-GRS	6	+ Read access to secondary	Reporting off secondary region
GZRS / RA-GZRS	6	Zonal + geo-redundant	Mission-critical global apps

Choosing the Right Redundancy

- **LRS**: Lowest cost, but no protection from datacenter failure
- **ZRS**: High availability within region; use for web apps and disks
- **GRS/RA-GRS**: Protect against regional disasters; necessary for compliance
- **GZRS**: Combines zone and region failover; ideal for financial or medical systems

Note: You cannot change from LRS to ZRS once the storage account is created.

Data Consistency Models

AZURE STORAGE GUARANTEES **strong consistency** across all replication types:

- **Strong consistency** means that once a write operation is confirmed, any subsequent read will return the latest value, regardless of replication model.
- This allows for simpler application logic and is one of Azure's advantages over eventually consistent stores.

Geo-Replication Considerations

WITH GRS AND GZRS, your data is asynchronously replicated to a **paired Azure region**. The replication lag is generally a few minutes, and in a disaster, Microsoft can perform a **failover**.

Geo-Failover Process:

1. Azure detects permanent failure in the primary region.
2. Failover is initiated via customer or Microsoft.
3. DNS is repointed to secondary.
4. All read/write operations resume from the new primary.

CLI FAILOVER EXAMPLE:

az storage account failover—name mystorage—resource-group rg-prod

Note: After failover, you may lose some unreplicated writes. Use **Zone Redundant Storage (ZRS)** with **Geo Redundancy (GZRS)** to reduce this risk.

Designing for Read and Write Optimization

Read Optimization

- USE **Azure CDN** or **Front Door** to cache blob content globally.

- Enable **RA-GRS** for read access to a secondary region.
- Use **query acceleration** for selective access on large blobs.

Write Optimization

- DISTRIBUTE WRITES across partitions (especially in Table Storage or Cosmos DB).
- For append workloads, use **Append Blobs** to minimize locking.
- Use **Azure Event Grid** or **Service Bus** for write decoupling.

Access Control and Security

Access Mechanisms

- **Shared Access Signatures (SAS)**: Time-bound, scoped tokens
- **Azure AD RBAC**: Identity-based access for fine-grained control
- **Access Keys**: Account-level shared secrets (should be rotated regularly)

Recommendation:

- Use **Azure AD for service-to-service access**
- Avoid exposing keys or long-lived SAS tokens
- Enable **Soft Delete** and **Immutable Blob Policies** for critical data

Enable Soft Delete Example:

az storage blob service-properties delete-policy update \

—account-name mystorage \

—enable true \

—days-retained 30

Multi-Region Access and Performance

APPLICATIONS THAT NEED fast, global access to storage should adopt:

- **ZRS for regional availability**
- **GZRS + CDN** for worldwide replication and access
- **Front Door or Traffic Manager** for DNS-based routing
- **Premium storage** for low latency and high throughput

Use **Performance Testing** tools like AzCopy and Storage Performance Benchmarking Toolkit to validate design choices.

Azure Files Access Models

FOR APPLICATIONS REQUIRING file shares:

- **Azure Files (Standard)**: SMB over the internet/VNet
- **Azure Files (Premium)**: SMB/NFS on SSDs, high throughput

Mount via SMB:

net use Z: \\mystorage.file.core.windows.net\myshare /user:Azure\mystorage <storage-key>

Mount via NFS (Linux clients only):

- Available only for premium file shares
- Requires ADDS or Azure AD DS integration for identity

Cache, CDN, and Tiering

TO REDUCE LATENCY AND optimize bandwidth:

- Use **Azure CDN** to cache blob content near users
- Deploy **Azure File Sync** to tier between local servers and Azure Files
- Implement **Edge Zones** and **Cache for Azure Files** for branch office acceleration

---

Redundancy and High Availability Patterns

DESIGN HIGH-AVAILABILITY using these patterns:

Pattern	Description	Use Case
Active-Active Regions	Write/read to both regions	Multi-region SaaS platform
Active-Passive Failover	Primary write, secondary read until failover	Compliance-focused apps
Edge + Cloud Tiering	Cache data locally, store long-term in Azure	Branch office with limited bandwidth
Eventual Archiving	Auto-move blobs to Archive tier after 90 days	Long-term logs, invoices

Combine with automation (Logic Apps, Functions) for self-healing and retention.

Monitoring Data Access and Redundancy

ENABLE DIAGNOSTICS to track:

- **Read/write request volume**
- **Throttling and latency**

- **Geo-replication status**
- **Soft delete recovery events**
- **Access anomalies or blocked access attempts**

Use **Log Analytics** to run queries like:

```
AzureDiagnostics
| where ResourceType == "STORAGEACCOUNTS"
| where OperationName == "GetBlob"
| summarize count() by bin(TimeGenerated, 1h), CallerIpAddress
```

Set **Alerts** on anomaly detection or replication lag.

Summary

DESIGNING DATA ACCESS and redundancy models in Azure is essential to ensuring application resilience, performance, and security. The right strategy balances cost, availability, compliance, and operational simplicity.

Best Practices:

- Match storage redundancy with business continuity and SLA needs
- Use lifecycle policies to automate tiering based on access patterns
- Architect with strong consistency in mind to simplify logic
- Secure data with RBAC, SAS, and encryption
- Distribute access globally with GZRS, CDN, and Front Door

- Monitor access and redundancy health using Azure Monitor and Log Analytics

In the next section, we will address securing Azure storage using encryption, firewalls, private endpoints, and access control strategies to ensure your data remains protected across all layers of the architecture.

Securing Storage with Keys, Firewalls, and Private Endpoints

DATA SECURITY IS ONE of the most critical aspects of architecting storage solutions on Azure. As a Solutions Architect, you must design storage environments that prevent unauthorized access, protect sensitive data at rest and in transit, and comply with regulatory and organizational security standards. Azure provides a comprehensive set of security features, including encryption, access control, networking isolation, firewall configuration, and private endpoints.

This section explores how to secure Azure storage accounts using keys, Shared Access Signatures (SAS), role-based access control (RBAC), Azure Active Directory (AAD), firewalls, service endpoints, and private endpoints. It also examines best practices, compliance considerations, and how to monitor and audit storage security posture at scale.

Storage Account Security Layers

SECURING STORAGE INVOLVES applying controls at multiple levels:

1. **Identity & Access Control** (Who can access)
2. **Network Access Controls** (Where it can be accessed from)

3. **Data Protection** (How it is protected in transit and at rest)
4. **Auditing & Monitoring** (How it's monitored and verified)

Each layer contributes to a defense-in-depth strategy that hardens your storage infrastructure.

Access Control Mechanisms

AZURE SUPPORTS MULTIPLE access models:

1. Shared Keys

- EACH STORAGE ACCOUNT has two 512-bit access keys (primary and secondary).
- Full access to all resources in the account.
- Recommended only for trusted backend services and short-lived integrations.

Example (CLI):

az storage account keys list—account-name mystorage

Security Concern: If leaked, shared keys grant full control. Rotate keys frequently.

---

2. Shared Access Signatures (SAS)

SAS TOKENS PROVIDE granular, time-bound access to storage resources without exposing the primary keys.

Types of SAS:

- **Service SAS**: Grants access to specific services (Blob, File, Queue, Table).
- **Account SAS**: Grants access to all services in the storage account.
- **User Delegation SAS**: Uses Azure AD tokens for enhanced security.

Sample SAS Generation:

```
az storage blob generate-sas \
—account-name mystorage \
—container-name logs \
—name error.log \
—permissions r \
—expiry 2025-01-01T00:00Z \
—output tsv
```

Best Practices:

- Always set expiry on SAS tokens.
- Restrict permissions to the minimum required.
- Prefer **User Delegation SAS** over Account SAS when possible.

---

3. Azure Active Directory Integration

AZURE AD PROVIDES IDENTITY-based access via **role assignments**.

Benefits:

- Avoids shared secrets.
- Supports conditional access policies.
- Enables MFA and Just-in-Time access.

Common RBAC Roles:

Role	Description
Storage Blob Data Reader	Read blobs and containers
Storage Blob Data Contributor	Read/write/delete blobs
Storage Queue Data Contributor	Full access to queues

Assign Role (CLI):

```
az role assignment create \
—assignee user@contoso.com \
—role "Storage Blob Data Contributor" \
—scope
"/subscriptions/<sub-id>/resourceGroups/<rg>/providers/
Microsoft.Storage/storageAccounts/mystorage"
```

Use AAD when:

- Access is from within Azure (VMs, Functions).
- You need enterprise-grade identity control.

Network Security and Firewalls

CONTROLLING THE NETWORK path to your storage account prevents exposure to the public internet.

1. Azure Storage Firewall

THE STORAGE FIREWALL enables you to:

- Deny access by default
- Allow only specific **IP addresses** or **virtual networks**

Enable Firewall (CLI):

```
az storage account update \
—name mystorage \
—resource-group secure-rg \
—default-action Deny \
—bypass AzureServices \
—ip-rules 203.0.113.0/24 198.51.100.0/24
```

Best Practices:

- Block all internet traffic unless explicitly required.
- Use bypass for trusted Azure services (e.g., Azure Monitor).
- Combine with Private Endpoints where possible.

---

2. Service Endpoints

SERVICE ENDPOINTS ALLOW you to extend your VNet to Azure Storage without exposing it publicly.

Use Case: Access from VMs or apps in a subnet without routing over the public internet.

Limitations:

- Still resolves to public IP
- Does not prevent public access by default

Enable on Subnet (CLI):

```
az network vnet subnet update \
—name appsubnet \
—vnet-name appvnet \
—resource-group network-rg \
—service-endpoints Microsoft.Storage
```

---

3. Private Endpoints

PRIVATE ENDPOINTS ARE the most secure way to connect to Azure Storage.

- Assigns a private IP from your VNet to the storage account.
- Traffic remains entirely within the Azure backbone.
- Completely disables public internet access if configured with firewall rules.

Create Private Endpoint (CLI):

```
az network private-endpoint create \
—name pe-storage \
—resource-group secure-rg \
```

—vnet-name prod-vnet \

—subnet subnet-secure \

—private-connection-resource-id "/subscriptions/xxx/resourceGroups/rg/providers/Microsoft.Storage/storageAccounts/mystorage" \

—group-id blob

Key Design Tips:

- Use DNS zone privatelink.blob.core.windows.net to resolve private IPs.
- Use Private Endpoints for all production workloads.
- Ensure **NSGs** and **UDRs** allow traffic to and from private IPs.

Data Protection and Encryption

AZURE STORAGE ENCRYPTS all data at rest by default using Microsoft-managed keys.

Encryption Models:

Encryption Type	Description
Server-Side Encryption (SSE)	Default for all Azure Storage types
Customer-Managed Keys (CMK)	Use your own keys stored in Key Vault
Double Encryption	Applies both platform and customer keys
Client-Side Encryption	Encrypt data before uploading (custom)

ENABLE CMK (PORTAL/CLI):

az storage account update \

—name mystorage \

—resource-group secure-rg \

—encryption-key-source Microsoft.Keyvault \

—encryption-key-vault uri=https://mykeyvault.vault.azure.net/ key-name=key1

Immutable Storage and Soft Delete

AZURE PROVIDES **immutability policies** for regulatory compliance:

- **Time-based Retention**: Lock blob for a fixed period (WORM)
- **Legal Hold**: Prevents deletion until hold is removed

Enable Policy (CLI):

az storage container immutability-policy create \

—account-name mystorage \

—container-name records \

—period 365 \

—allow-protected-append-writes true

Enable **Soft Delete** for recovery from accidental deletions:

- Blobs
- File Shares

• Containers

Monitoring, Auditing, and Alerts

SECURITY IS INCOMPLETE without visibility. Monitor the following:

- **Access logs**: Who accessed what and when
- **Anomalies**: Unusual access patterns
- **Permission changes**: RBAC or SAS modifications
- **Threat detections**: Alerts from Microsoft Defender for Storage

Enable Diagnostic Settings:

```
az monitor diagnostic-settings create \
—resource "/subscriptions/xxx/resourceGroups/rg/providers/Microsoft.Storage/storageAccounts/mystorage" \
—workspace "/subscriptions/xxx/resourceGroups/monitoring-rg/providers/Microsoft.OperationalInsights/workspaces/logs" \
—logs '[{"category": "StorageRead", "enabled": true}]'
```

KQL for Access Events:

```
AzureDiagnostics
| where ResourceType == "STORAGEACCOUNTS"
| where OperationName contains "GetBlob"
| summarize count() by CallerIpAddress, bin(TimeGenerated, 1h)
```

Set alerts for:

- Access from unknown IPs
- Use of shared keys
- SAS token overuse

Compliance and Security Benchmarks

AZURE STORAGE CAN BE configured to meet:

- **HIPAA**
- **ISO 27001**
- **SOC 2**
- **GDPR**
- **NIST 800-53**

Use tools like:

- **Microsoft Defender for Cloud** to assess security posture
- **Azure Policy** to enforce encryption, firewall rules, and tagging
- **Azure Blueprints** to automate secure deployment patterns

---

Summary

SECURING AZURE STORAGE involves designing layered protections across identity, access, network, and data planes. Your architecture must balance performance and usability with stringent compliance and enterprise security requirements.

Security Best Practices for Architects:

- Use **Azure AD RBAC** instead of account keys where possible

- Prefer **User Delegation SAS** for token-based access
- Restrict public access and enforce **Private Endpoints**
- Configure **Storage Firewall and VNet Rules**
- Encrypt using **Customer-Managed Keys** for compliance-sensitive data
- Enable **Soft Delete** and **Immutability Policies**
- Monitor access with **Azure Monitor Logs** and configure **security alerts**

In the next section, we will explore how to integrate multiple Azure storage solutions—Blob Storage, File Shares, and Data Lake—into cohesive architectures that support enterprise-scale data movement, analytics, and operations.

Integrating Azure Files, Blob Storage, and Data Lake

ENTERPRISE APPLICATIONS rarely operate with a single type of data or storage requirement. A modern cloud architecture must integrate multiple Azure storage solutions to meet diverse use cases ranging from user uploads, document repositories, shared file systems, analytic pipelines, to machine learning and AI workloads. Microsoft Azure provides a variety of data services including **Blob Storage**, **Azure Files**, and **Azure Data Lake Storage Gen2**, each optimized for specific usage patterns. However, to deliver holistic solutions, these services must be interconnected into a unified data strategy.

In this section, we will explore the architectural principles, patterns, and implementation strategies for integrating Azure Files, Blob

Storage, and Data Lake into comprehensive solutions. We'll cover data movement techniques, hybrid access, synchronization models, analytics integration, performance considerations, and best practices.

Overview of Storage Services

Azure Blob Storage

- OPTIMIZED FOR UNSTRUCTURED object storage
- Supports hot, cool, archive tiers
- Common uses: user uploads, logs, backups, images, videos

Azure Files

- MANAGED FILE SHARES accessible via SMB and NFS
- Can be mounted on Windows, Linux, and macOS
- Ideal for lift-and-shift scenarios, legacy apps, and shared file access

Azure Data Lake Storage Gen2 (ADLS Gen2)

- BUILT ON TOP OF Blob Storage with hierarchical namespace
- Adds POSIX permissions, directory-level control
- Optimized for analytics and big data processing

Selecting the Right Storage for the Task

Use Case	Recommended Service
Web/mobile app file uploads	Blob Storage
Shared configuration and logs	Azure Files
Analytics staging area	ADLS Gen2
Legacy apps needing mapped drives	Azure Files
Machine learning feature store	ADLS Gen2
Image and video repositories	Blob Storage
Data lake for Power BI/Synapse	ADLS Gen2

BEST PRACTICE: Design storage solutions to specialize per workload and **integrate at the access or data orchestration layer**.

Cross-Service Integration Patterns

1. Ingest → Store → Process

A COMMON PATTERN IN data pipelines involves ingesting files from users or systems, storing them in raw format, and processing them later.

Pattern Flow:

- **Blob Storage** or **Azure Files** for initial ingestion
- Use **Azure Data Factory (ADF)** to copy data into **ADLS Gen2**
- Process data using **Azure Synapse, Databricks**, or **HDInsight**

Example: Move Blob Data to ADLS

az datafactory pipeline create \

—factory-name myfactory \

—resource-group data-rg \

—name ingestPipeline \

—pipeline "@pipeline.json"

---

2. Shared File and Data Lake Access

YOU MAY NEED BOTH USER-level access to files and analytics access to large data volumes.

Scenario:

- Application writes logs and documents to **Azure Files**
- Azure Data Factory or Logic Apps sync the file share into **ADLS Gen2** nightly for analysis

Sync Strategy:

- Use **AzCopy**, **Azure File Sync**, or custom scripts with **Data Movement Library**

---

3. Metadata in Files, Content in Blobs

STORING STRUCTURED metadata in one storage system and binary files in another improves query performance.

Pattern:

- Store metadata (file name, upload time, user ID, tags) in **Azure Table Storage** or **Cosmos DB**
- Store content (e.g., PDFs, media) in **Blob Storage**

- Enable querying and filtering via metadata engine, while fetching actual content from Blob

Use Case: Document management systems, medical imaging archives

---

Connecting Storage Services to Analytics

Azure Synapse Analytics

- NATIVELY INTEGRATES with **ADLS Gen2** using **Synapse Workspace**
- Supports serverless SQL querying directly over files (CSV, Parquet)

```
SELECT *
FROM OPENROWSET(
BULK 'https://mydatalake.dfs.core.windows.net/raw-data/sales.csv',
FORMAT = 'CSV',
PARSER_VERSION = '2.0'
) AS [result]
```

Azure Data Explorer (ADX)

- INTEGRATES WITH Blob and ADLS via **data ingestion pipelines**
- Useful for real-time telemetry analysis and log aggregation

Power BI

- CONNECTS DIRECTLY to ADLS for large-scale analytics
- Dataflows can pull from Blob or Files using Azure connectors

Access and Identity Integration

CONSISTENT IDENTITY management across storage services is essential.

- Use **Azure AD** to manage access via RBAC or ACLs
- For **ADLS Gen2**, use **POSIX ACLs** for directory-level control

```
az storage fs access set \
—path "/data/teamA" \
—acl "user:userid:rwx,group:groupid:r-x,other::—-" \
—account-name datalakeaccount
```

For shared file access:

- Integrate **Azure Files** with **Azure AD DS** or **on-prem AD**
- Use **identity-based access** instead of storage keys

Hybrid Access and On-Prem Integration

MANY ENTERPRISES OPERATE in a hybrid environment. Azure provides multiple services to synchronize between on-premises and cloud storage.

Azure File Sync

- SYNCS ON-PREM FOLDERS with Azure Files
- Provides cloud tiering to offload infrequently used data

ExpressRoute or VPN

- FOR SECURE, HIGH-speed access to Blob and Files
- Use **Private Endpoints** for isolation

ADLS Hybrid Access

- FOR ADLS GEN2, INGEST on-prem files via **Data Box**, **AzCopy**, or **File Gateway**
- Schedule nightly uploads to maintain freshness of the lake

Performance and Optimization Techniques

Blob Storage

- USE **block blobs** for uploads
- Use **container-level access policies**
- Enable **blob versioning** and **soft delete**

Azure Files

- PREMIUM TIER FOR high IOPS
- Cache shares on VMs using **Azure File Sync**

ADLS Gen2

- PARTITION DATA USING folders for performance (e.g., /year=2025/month=01/)
- Use **Parquet** format for optimized reads in Synapse and Databricks
- Enable **recursive ACLs** for multi-level access control

Monitoring and Logging Across Services

ENABLE DIAGNOSTIC SETTINGS for each storage service:

- Route logs to **Log Analytics**
- Track **read/write/delete events**
- Alert on permission changes or anomalous access

Sample KQL Query:

```
AzureDiagnostics

| where ResourceType == "STORAGEACCOUNTS"

| where OperationName contains "Write"

| summarize count() by bin(TimeGenerated, 1h), Resource
```

Create unified **workbooks** that show metrics across Blob, Files, and ADLS for operational dashboards.

Security Integration

APPLY COMMON SECURITY controls across all services:

- **Private Endpoints** for VNet isolation

- **Azure Defender for Storage** for anomaly detection
- **Encryption at rest and in transit**
- **Azure Policy** to enforce diagnostics, tags, and key management

Automation and DevOps Integration

AUTOMATE PROVISIONING and integration using **Bicep** or **Terraform**.

Example Bicep for Blob + ADLS:

```
resource storage 'Microsoft.Storage/storageAccounts@2022-09-01' = {

name: 'storagedev'

location: resourceGroup().location

sku: {

name: 'Standard_LRS'

}

kind: 'StorageV2'

properties: {

isHnsEnabled: true // Enables Data Lake Gen2

}

}
```

Automate **sync pipelines** using **Azure DevOps**, **Logic Apps**, or **Data Factory triggers.**

Summary

MODERN CLOUD ARCHITECTURES demand multi-modal storage strategies that combine the capabilities of Blob Storage, Azure Files, and Azure Data Lake. Rather than choosing one service, architects must design **integrated data systems** that align each component to the role it performs best.

Integration Best Practices:

- Use Blob for media, backups, static content
- Use Azure Files for legacy apps and user sharing
- Use ADLS Gen2 for analytics and large-scale structured data
- Sync data between services using ADF, AzCopy, and pipelines
- Apply consistent security controls and monitoring across all tiers
- Optimize format (Parquet, CSV), partitioning, and tiering for performance and cost
- Automate deployment and data movement via infrastructure as code

In the next section, we'll explore how to design storage architectures for compliance with data retention policies, archiving strategies, and regulatory requirements like GDPR and HIPAA.

Designing for Data Archiving and Retention Policies

DATA ARCHIVING AND retention are fundamental concerns in enterprise cloud architecture. As organizations grow, so do their data volumes, regulatory obligations, and long-term storage needs. Azure offers several built-in features and architectural patterns that enable efficient, compliant, and cost-effective long-term data retention and archiving strategies.

In this section, we will explore the core principles of archiving, data classification strategies, regulatory compliance requirements, Azure-native services and tools, automation techniques for lifecycle management, and architectural patterns that enable secure and scalable data retention.

Understanding Data Archiving vs Retention

DATA ARCHIVING refers to the process of moving infrequently accessed data to long-term storage, often with the goal of reducing costs while preserving the data for future reference or legal requirements.

Data Retention defines how long data must be kept, often based on business or legal policies, after which it may be deleted, moved, or further archived.

Attribute	Archiving	Retention
Purpose	Cost savings, reduce operational storage load	Compliance, audit, legal obligations
Access Frequency	Rare	Defined by policy
Duration	Indefinite or multi-year	Typically fixed (e.g., 7 years)
Performance Needs	Low	Low
Tier	Cool / Archive	Hot / Cool / Archive
Storage Type	Azure Blob, Azure Files	Azure Blob, Tables, SQL, etc.

Legal and Regulatory Drivers

DATA RETENTION REQUIREMENTS are often driven by laws and standards:

Regulation/ Standard	Retention Period Example	Applies To
GDPR	"As long as necessary"	EU personal data
HIPAA	6 years	Medical records and health data
FINRA/SEC	7 years	Financial data and trade records
IRS (US)	7+ years	Tax documents
PCI-DSS	1–3 years	Cardholder data
ISO 27001	Based on business need	General information security management

Designing storage to meet these obligations includes ensuring **immutability**, **access auditing**, and **controlled deletion**.

Azure Blob Storage Tiers for Archiving

BLOB STORAGE OFFERS a cost-effective solution for archiving using its tiering system:

Hot Tier

- HIGHEST COST
- Instant access
- For active, frequently used data

Cool Tier

- LOWER STORAGE COST, higher access cost
- Minimum retention: 30 days
- For infrequent access but short-term retrieval needs

Archive Tier

- LOWEST COST
- Offline access model (rehydration required)
- Minimum retention: 180 days
- Rehydration time: up to 15 hours

Use Case: Regulatory document storage, legacy logs, historical records, scientific datasets

---

Automating Retention with Lifecycle Management

AZURE STORAGE SUPPORTS lifecycle management policies that automate blob tiering and deletion based on age or last modified date.

Sample Lifecycle Policy (JSON):

```
{
"rules": [
{
"name": "archive-after-90-delete-after-730",
```

```
"enabled": true,
"definition": {
"filters": {
"blobTypes": ["blockBlob"],
"prefixMatch": ["archive-data/"]
},
"actions": {
"baseBlob": {
"tierToArchive": {
"daysAfterModificationGreaterThan": 90
},
"delete": {
"daysAfterModificationGreaterThan": 730
}
}
}
}
}
]
}
```

CLI to Apply:

az storage account management-policy create \

—account-name mystorage \

—policy "@policy.json" \

—resource-group rg-storage

Immutability and WORM Policies

AZURE SUPPORTS **immutable blob storage**, allowing you to enforce Write Once Read Many (WORM) behavior.

Use Cases:

- Legal hold requirements
- SEC 17a-4 compliance
- Chain-of-custody record keeping

Retention Modes:

- **Time-based retention**: Prevent deletion/modification for a defined period
- **Legal hold**: Indefinite lock until explicitly removed

Example CLI to Enable Immutability:

az storage container immutability-policy create \

—account-name mystorage \

—container-name records \

—period 365 \

—allow-protected-append-writes true

Note: Once locked, data cannot be deleted even by administrators.

Designing for Tiered Access Models

COMBINE BLOB STORAGE tiers with a tiered access design:

1. **Hot Tier**: 0–30 days (operational, active processing)
2. **Cool Tier**: 31–90 days (reference, compliance checks)
3. **Archive Tier**: 91+ days (long-term, legal)

Use **lifecycle policies** to automate transitions and save costs over time.

Sample Timeline Strategy:

Time After Upload	Action
30 days	Move to cool tier
90 days	Move to archive tier
2 years	Delete blob permanently

Archiving Non-Blob Data

Azure Files

- CURRENTLY NO ARCHIVE tier
- For long-term file archiving, use **Azure File Sync + Azure Blob**
- Or migrate file shares to Blob storage for cheaper storage using **AzCopy**

Azure SQL Database

USE **long-term backup retention (LTR)** for databases:

- Store full backups in RA-GRS blob storage
- Retention up to 10 years
- Automated via configuration

```
az sql db ltr-policy set \
—resource-group rg \
—server sqlserver \
—database prod \
—weekly-retention P10Y
```

Azure Table Storage

NO BUILT-IN LIFECYCLE policies. Archive by exporting to Blob or Cosmos DB or using a time-to-live (TTL) property in your schema.

Data Movement and Export for Archiving

AZURE SUPPORTS MULTIPLE tools and services to migrate or export data into archival storage:

Tool/Service	Use Case
AzCopy	Command-line tool for large data movement
Data Factory	Scheduled ETL and archiving jobs
Event Grid + Functions	Triggered archiving on blob creation
Logic Apps	Business-rule-based retention workflows
Data Box	Bulk offline transfer

Example Workflow:

- New document uploaded to Blob
- Event Grid triggers Azure Function
- Function applies metadata and moves older documents to archive tier

---

Hybrid and Edge Considerations

FOR HYBRID WORKLOADS:

- Use **Azure File Sync** to replicate on-prem folders to Azure
- Apply lifecycle and retention policies in the cloud
- For government or air-gapped scenarios, use **Data Box Heavy** to archive offline

---

Security and Compliance Integration

ENSURE ARCHIVED DATA is protected:

- Enable **encryption at rest** (Microsoft or Customer Managed Keys)

- Use **Private Endpoints** to prevent public access
- Apply **Azure Policy** to enforce tagging, region, and immutability

Policy Example: Deny storage accounts without immutability enabled

```
{
"if": {
"allOf": [
{
"field": "type",
"equals": "Microsoft.Storage/storageAccounts"
},
{
"field": "Microsoft.Storage/storageAccounts/supportsHttpsTrafficOnly",
"equals": "false"
}
]
},
"then": {
"effect": "deny"
}
```

}

Monitoring and Cost Optimization

USE **Azure Monitor** and **Cost Management** to track:

- Storage consumption by tier
- Retention duration per container
- Cost trends over time

Recommendations:

- Use **RA-GRS Archive** for mission-critical long-term data
- Avoid storing inactive data in Hot tier
- Export reports for audit compliance

Summary

DESIGNING FOR DATA archiving and retention in Azure is about finding the right balance between compliance, accessibility, cost, and operational simplicity. Azure provides the tools to meet nearly any regulatory requirement while optimizing storage usage through automated policies and intelligent tiering.

Key Architect Practices:

- Use lifecycle management for automated tiering and deletion
- Leverage archive tiers for deep storage cost savings
- Apply immutability policies to enforce compliance (WORM)
- Integrate Function apps or Logic Apps for intelligent archiving

- Ensure all archived data is encrypted and access-controlled
- Monitor tier usage and implement retention policies across all services

With these strategies in place, you can confidently build long-term data retention architectures that are efficient, auditable, and future-ready. In the next chapter, we will explore how to design for business continuity and disaster recovery across all critical workloads in the Azure cloud.

Chapter 4: Designing Business Continuity and Disaster Recovery Strategies

Defining RPO and RTO Requirements

IN ANY ENTERPRISE-GRADE architecture, the ability to recover from failures—whether caused by hardware malfunctions, human error, natural disasters, or malicious attacks—is essential. Designing for **Business Continuity** (BC) and **Disaster Recovery** (**DR**) requires a clear understanding of the business impact of downtime and data loss. This begins with defining two fundamental metrics: **Recovery Point Objective** (**RPO**) and **Recovery Time Objective** (**RTO**).

These metrics dictate how tolerant an organization is to interruptions and data loss and guide all subsequent architectural and tooling decisions. This section explores how to define, interpret, and apply RPO and RTO to Azure-based architectures, with practical techniques to classify workloads, align service capabilities, and implement cost-effective, compliant BC/DR strategies.

Understanding RPO and RTO

Recovery Point Objective (RPO)

RPO IS THE **maximum acceptable amount of data loss** measured in time. It reflects how much data your organization can afford to lose in the event of an incident.

- **Example**: If your RPO is 15 minutes, your backups or replicas must capture data at least every 15 minutes.

• **Impact**: Influences how frequently backups or data synchronization should occur.

Recovery Time Objective (RTO)

RTO IS THE **maximum acceptable amount of time** to restore operations after a failure.

• **Example**: If your RTO is 2 hours, all services and systems must be back online within 2 hours of a disruption.

• **Impact**: Dictates architectural decisions for failover, replication, and automation.

Visualizing RPO and RTO in a Timeline

CONSIDER A TIMELINE for a mission-critical application:

• 9:00 AM – Last backup taken

• 9:10 AM – System failure occurs

• 9:30 AM – Recovery starts

• 10:00 AM – Recovery completes

• **RPO** = 10 minutes (data created between 9:00 and 9:10 lost)

• **RTO** = 30 minutes (time taken to restore service)

The tighter the RPO/RTO requirements, the more robust and costly the solution becomes.

Mapping Business Requirements to RPO/RTO

TO DEFINE RPO AND RTO, engage with business stakeholders:

- Identify **critical business functions** (e.g., payments, customer onboarding)
- Determine **acceptable downtime** and **data loss tolerance**
- Align with **regulatory requirements** (e.g., GDPR, HIPAA)
- Classify systems as:
    - **Mission-Critical** (seconds to minutes)
    - **Important** (hours)
    - **Non-Critical** (days)

Sample Workload Classification Table:

System	RPO	RTO	Classification
Online Banking	≤ 5 minutes	≤ 15 minutes	Mission-Critical
HR Management	1 hour	4 hours	Important
Development Portal	24 hours	2 days	Non-Critical

Azure Services and Their RPO/RTO Capabilities

AZURE OFFERS A VARIETY of services with built-in or configurable BC/DR features. Choosing the right ones depends on your RPO/RTO targets.

Compute

- **Azure Virtual Machines**:
    - Use **Azure Backup** for RPO of ~12–24 hours
    - Use **Azure Site Recovery (ASR)** for RPO of ~5–15 minutes and RTO of minutes

- **Azure App Services**:
  - Support deployment slots and regional redundancy
  - Geo-redundant traffic routing with Front Door or Traffic Manager

Storage

- **Azure Storage**:
  - Choose **ZRS** or **GZRS** for zone and geo-resiliency
  - Enable **versioning** and **soft delete** to reduce data loss
- **Azure SQL Database**:
  - Built-in geo-replication for automatic failover
  - Point-in-time restore for 7–35 days of backup history

Data Platforms

Service	Backup Options	Replication	Failover
Azure SQL Database	Point-in-time restore, LTR	Geo-Replication	Auto
Cosmos DB	TTL + Multi-region writes	Multi-master or passive	Auto
Azure Blob Storage	Snapshots + Lifecycle Policies	RA-GRS, GZRS	Manual

Defining RPO and RTO with Stakeholders

1. **Identify Critical Data and Applications**
   Engage with business units to inventory applications and databases.
2. **Define Impact Thresholds**
   What's the cost of 15 minutes of downtime? Of 1 hour of data loss?
3. **Create a BC/DR Matrix**
   Use a matrix to categorize and align each system with its RPO and RTO.
4. **Document and Validate**
   Record requirements in architectural documentation and validate through tabletop exercises or failover simulations.

Design Patterns to Meet RPO/RTO

Active-Active

- BOTH REGIONS HANDLE production traffic
- Ideal for applications needing near-zero RTO
- Requires distributed writes (e.g., Cosmos DB, custom replication)

Use Case: Global e-commerce platform with 24/7 uptime

Active-Passive (Hot Standby)

- PRIMARY REGION HANDLES traffic; secondary is replicated and ready
- Failover is either automatic or manual

- Suitable for moderate RTO (~15 minutes)

Use Case: ERP system with nightly data sync and DR drills

Backup and Restore

- REGULAR BACKUPS stored in geo-redundant storage
- Recovery process requires manual data rehydration and redeployment
- High RPO and RTO

Use Case: Dev/test workloads or archival systems

Example RPO/RTO-Driven Architecture

SCENARIO: A financial services application handling real-time transactions

Requirement	Design Choice
RPO: ≤ 5 min	Continuous replication via **Azure Site Recovery**
RTO: ≤ 15 min	Pre-provisioned compute in secondary region
DB replication	Active geo-replication in **Azure SQL**
DNS failover	**Azure Traffic Manager** with priority routing
Storage resilience	Use of **RA-GRS** or **GZRS** for blob storage

Failover Drill Plan:

- Validate replication status
- Test DNS switch
- Validate data integrity
- Log time to recover and validate against RTO

Cost vs Resiliency Trade-Offs

TIGHTER RPO/RTO COMES with higher costs:

Strategy	RPO	RTO	Relative Cost
Backup Only	Hours–days	Hours	$
Active-Passive	~15 min	~15 min	$$
Active-Active	Seconds	Seconds	$$$

Recommendation: Align RPO/RTO with business criticality to optimize cost.

Testing and Validation

DESIGNS ARE ONLY AS good as their tested outcomes.

Validation Techniques:

- **Tabletop Exercises**: Simulate disaster scenarios
- **Full DR Drills**: Failover to secondary, test recovery workflows
- **Chaos Engineering**: Induce controlled failures to test assumptions
- **Monitoring**: Log replication delays, backup failures, and DR readiness

Key Metrics:

- RPO compliance rate
- RTO adherence rate
- Mean Time To Recover (MTTR)
- Recovery audit logs

Governance and Documentation

GOVERNANCE PRACTICES include:

- Versioned BC/DR plans
- Ownership roles (e.g., DR lead, application owner)
- Change management (test after significant infrastructure changes)
- Integration into InfoSec and compliance reporting

Documentation must contain:

- Defined RPO/RTO for every workload
- Mapped services and regions
- Contact lists
- Failover and failback procedures
- Escalation paths

Summary

DEFINING AND ARCHITECTING for RPO and RTO is foundational to designing robust, resilient, and compliant cloud solutions. These metrics are the lens through which every BC/DR decision must be evaluated. Azure provides a rich set of capabilities—from backup to replication to active-active deployment models—that empower architects to meet stringent business demands.

Architectural Practices Summary:

- Collaborate with stakeholders to define clear RPO/RTO

- Classify applications by business criticality
- Match Azure services and replication models to each workload
- Balance cost and complexity with realistic risk tolerance
- Automate and validate failover processes frequently
- Continuously monitor and document compliance with DR objectives

In the next section, we'll focus on building architectures that ensure high availability and seamless failover scenarios across zones and regions using Azure-native technologies.

Architecting High Availability and Failover Scenarios

HIGH AVAILABILITY (HA) and failover are core design principles for ensuring that applications remain operational even during unexpected infrastructure failures, maintenance activities, or regional outages. In Microsoft Azure, architects can leverage built-in redundancy features, zone and region-aware services, intelligent traffic routing, and self-healing patterns to maintain availability and deliver uninterrupted user experiences.

This section explores the architecture, strategies, and tooling necessary to build highly available solutions on Azure. We'll examine zonal and regional architectures, service-specific HA patterns, traffic management techniques, monitoring integrations, and recovery automation. The goal is to help you confidently design robust failover mechanisms that align with your RTO (Recovery Time Objective) and SLA targets.

Principles of High Availability in Azure

HIGH AVAILABILITY IS defined as the ability of a system to remain operational and accessible during component or service failures.

Key Design Principles:

- **Redundancy**: Duplicate critical components across fault boundaries.
- **Isolation**: Ensure fault domains are isolated to prevent cascading failures.
- **Automated Recovery**: Use health probes and automation for fast detection and recovery.
- **Elasticity**: Scale resources dynamically to handle demand surges or instance failures.
- **Geographic Distribution**: Spread across zones and regions for maximum resilience.

Target Metrics:

- **Uptime SLAs**: Expressed as percentages (e.g., 99.99% = ~4.4 min/month downtime).
- **Mean Time to Recovery (MTTR)**: Average time to restore after failure.
- **Service Level Objectives (SLOs)**: Internal targets that map to SLAs.

Fault Domains and Update Domains

IN AZURE, VMS AND CERTAIN platform services are deployed across **Fault Domains (FDs)** and **Update Domains (UDs)** to ensure availability during hardware failures or maintenance.

- **Fault Domain**: Group of resources sharing a common power source and network switch.
- **Update Domain**: Group of resources updated at the same time during patching.

Availability Sets automatically distribute VMs across multiple FDs and UDs within a datacenter.

```
az vm availability-set create \

—name app-avset \

—resource-group rg-ha \

—platform-fault-domain-count 2 \

—platform-update-domain-count 5
```

Use Case: Ensure 99.95% SLA for VMs by deploying in an availability set.

Zonal Architecture: Availability Zones

AVAILABILITY ZONES (AZs) are physically separate datacenters within an Azure region. Each zone has independent power, cooling, and networking.

Benefits:

- Protection against datacenter-level failures

- SLA of 99.99% when deployed across zones

How to Use:

- Deploy VMs in **Availability Zones** via zone-aware scale sets.
- Use **Zone-redundant services** (e.g., ZRS Storage, Standard Load Balancer).

Example:

az vm create \

—name webvm1 \

—resource-group rg-web \

—zone 1 \

—image UbuntuLTS \

—admin-username azureuser

Common Zonal Services:

Service	Zone-Aware Options Available
Virtual Machines	Yes (manual or scale set)
Azure Kubernetes Service	Yes
App Gateway	Yes
Storage (ZRS, GZRS)	Yes
Cosmos DB	Yes (multi-region)
SQL Database	Zone-redundant configuration

Regional Resiliency and Geo-Pairing

IF ZONE-LEVEL HA IS insufficient (e.g., natural disasters, regional outages), deploy across **Azure paired regions**.

- Each Azure region is paired with another within the same geography.
- Updates are staggered to minimize regional impact.
- Recommended for BCDR and regulatory compliance.

Design Considerations:

- Replicate databases and storage to secondary region (RA-GRS, geo-replication).
- Deploy active/passive or active/active application tiers in both regions.
- Use **Azure Traffic Manager** or **Front Door** for failover routing.

Failover Routing and Load Balancing

FAILOVER MECHANISMS are triggered by **health probes**, which monitor endpoint availability and redirect traffic as needed.

Azure Load Balancer

- OPERATES AT LAYER 4 (TCP/UDP)
- Offers **zone-redundant configurations**
- Used for internal and public-facing traffic

Azure Application Gateway

- LAYER 7 (HTTP/HTTPS) load balancer with **Web Application Firewall (WAF)**
- Zone-aware

- Supports session affinity and SSL offloading

Azure Front Door

- GLOBAL ENTRY POINT with **geo-aware routing**
- Fast failover using health probes
- SSL termination, WAF, and URL path routing

Azure Traffic Manager

- DNS-BASED TRAFFIC routing
- Priority, Weighted, and Geographic routing methods
- Slower failover (~20–30 seconds due to DNS TTL)

Failover Setup with Traffic Manager:

```
az network traffic-manager profile create \
—name myapp-profile \
—resource-group rg-ha \
—routing-method Priority \
—unique-dns-name myapp-traffic \
—ttl 30 \
—monitor-path "/health"
```

High Availability by Service

Azure App Service

- SUPPORTS DEPLOYMENT slots and regional redundancy
- Use **App Service Environment (ASE)** for isolated, high-scale environments
- Use **App Service backups** and **auto-scale rules**

Azure Kubernetes Service (AKS)

- DEPLOY ACROSS **Availability Zones**
- Use **PodDisruptionBudgets**, **node pools**, and **auto-scaler**
- Integrate with **Azure Load Balancer** or **Application Gateway Ingress Controller**

Azure SQL Database

- ENABLE **Zone-Redundant Configuration**
- Use **Auto-failover Groups** for cross-region HA

Azure Cosmos DB

- MULTI-REGION WRITES or reads
- Automatic failover with consistency policies (e.g., Session, Strong)

az cosmosdb update \

—name mycosmos \

—resource-group rg-db \

—failover-policies eastus westus

Active-Active vs Active-Passive Patterns

Active-Active

- USERS ARE ROUTED to the nearest healthy region
- All regions actively serve traffic
- Use for read-heavy or globally distributed workloads

Example: Cosmos DB with multi-region writes and Front Door routing

Active-Passive

- TRAFFIC GOES TO primary until failure occurs
- Secondary region is warm standby
- Simpler to manage and more cost-efficient

Example: SQL failover group with App Service standby in paired region

---

Health Probes and Application Monitoring

HEALTH PROBES ARE CRITICAL for detecting failures and triggering failover:

- Use **Azure Monitor Application Insights** for detailed telemetry

- Configure health endpoints (/health) for load balancers and DNS routers
- Set up **Log Analytics alerts** to detect issues before SLA impact

KQL Query Example:

```
requests
| where success == false
| summarize errorCount = count() by bin(timestamp, 5m)
```

Testing High Availability and Failover

TESTING IS ESSENTIAL for validating HA architectures:

- Perform **planned failover drills**
- Simulate **region unavailability** using traffic blocking or Azure Chaos Studio
- Use synthetic probes to test health endpoint reliability
- Track **failover time**, **availability gaps**, and **response latency**

Cost Optimization and Trade-Offs

WHILE HIGH AVAILABILITY improves reliability, it increases cost and complexity. Balance trade-offs based on workload criticality.

HA Level	RTO	RPO	Relative Cost
Basic redundancy	Hours	Hours	$
Zonal	Minutes	Near zero	$$
Geo-resilient	Seconds	Near zero	$$$

Architectural Guidance:

- Use ZRS storage and zone-aware services as default for production
- Enable geo-replication selectively for mission-critical services
- Automate cost-saving scale-in during low-demand hours

Summary

ARCHITECTING FOR HIGH availability and failover in Azure involves a comprehensive strategy across compute, networking, storage, and application layers. Leveraging built-in features like availability zones, traffic routing, and service redundancy allows you to meet strict uptime SLAs and deliver continuous service to users—even during failure events.

Architect's Checklist:

- Use **Availability Sets or Zones** for intra-region resilience
- Deploy **active-passive or active-active** models based on business needs
- Integrate **Azure Load Balancer, Traffic Manager, or Front Door** for routing
- Replicate data using geo-redundant services like RA-GRS or Cosmos DB
- Implement **health probes and monitoring** for early detection and automation
- Test failover scenarios regularly and document MTTR metrics

In the next section, we'll examine how to use Azure-native backup services and recovery automation to build comprehensive recovery strategies for virtual machines, databases, and PaaS services.

Implementing Azure Backup and Site Recovery

A ROBUST CLOUD ARCHITECTURE must account for unexpected failures, data loss, ransomware, and system corruption. While high availability ensures continuous operation, it does not eliminate the need for reliable **backup** and **disaster recovery (DR)** mechanisms. Microsoft Azure provides two powerful services—**Azure Backup** and **Azure Site Recovery (ASR)**—designed to protect your data and applications, minimize recovery time, and meet compliance requirements.

In this section, we will explore how to design, implement, and manage backup and DR strategies using Azure-native tools. You'll learn about backup vaults, recovery policies, DR replication models, supported workloads, automation techniques, monitoring best practices, and how to test and validate recovery plans in a controlled and scalable way.

Understanding Azure Backup vs Azure Site Recovery

Feature	Azure Backup	Azure Site Recovery
Purpose	Data protection	Workload replication and failover
Target	Files, VMs, SQL, SAP HANA, Azure Blobs	VMs (Azure and on-prem), physical servers
Recovery Time Objective	Minutes to hours	Seconds to minutes
Recovery Point Objective	Hours (or less with enhanced policies)	Minutes
Use Case	Recovery from accidental deletion, corruption	Failover during site outage or disaster

KEY INSIGHT: Backup protects data, while Site Recovery preserves continuity of operations.

Azure Backup Architecture

AZURE BACKUP IS A PAAS offering built on the **Azure Recovery Services Vault**, which stores backup metadata and recovery points.

Supported Workloads:

- AZURE VMS (WINDOWS and Linux)
- On-premises VMs (via MARS/MABS agents)
- SQL Server and SAP HANA on Azure VMs
- Azure File Shares

- Azure Blobs (via Backup Center preview)
- Azure PostgreSQL

Backup Vault Configuration:

AZ BACKUP VAULT CREATE \

—resource-group rg-backup \

—name backup-vault \

—location uksouth

Backup Policy Design

BACKUP POLICIES DEFINE the **frequency** and **retention** of backups.

Typical Azure VM Policy:

- Daily backup at 2 AM
- Retain daily backups for 30 days
- Retain weekly backups for 52 weeks
- Retain monthly backups for 12 months
- Retain yearly backups for 10 years

az backup policy create \

—vault-name backup-vault \

—name "long-retention" \

—resource-group rg-backup \

—backup-management-type AzureIaasVM \

—policy "@policy.json"

Best Practices:

- Use separate policies for dev, test, and prod environments.
- Align backup retention with regulatory compliance.
- Apply tags to vaults for cost and usage tracking.

Restoring Backups

AZURE BACKUP ALLOWS:

- **Full VM restore**: Create a new VM or replace existing
- **File-level recovery**: Mount restore point as a disk
- **Restore to alternate region** (cross-region restore with GRS)

CLI Example:

az backup restore restore-disks \

—resource-group rg-backup \

—vault-name backup-vault \

—container-name IaasVMContainer;iaasvmcontainerv2;vm01 \

—item-name vm01 \

—restore-to-staging-storage-account mystorage

Azure Site Recovery Architecture

AZURE SITE RECOVERY replicates workloads across **regions** or **between on-prem and Azure**, enabling automated **failover and failback**.

Key Components:

- **Recovery Services Vault**: Stores configuration and replication metadata
- **Process Server**: Intermediary for on-prem replication
- **Configuration Server**: Manages replication policies
- **Replication Policies**: Define RPO, frequency, and retention
- **Recovery Plans**: Orchestrate multi-VM failover

Supported Scenarios

Source	Target
Azure Region A	Azure Region B
On-prem VMware/Hyper-V	Azure Region
Physical Linux/Windows	Azure Region

SUPPORTED WORKLOADS:

- IaaS VMs
- Web Servers, Domain Controllers
- File Servers, Application Servers
- Database servers (SQL, Oracle, MySQL)

Configuring Azure Site Recovery

1. **Enable Site Recovery** in Recovery Services Vault
2. **Define Replication Policy**
3. **Select Source and Target**
4. **Enable Replication per VM**
5. **Create Recovery Plan** for grouped orchestration

AZ BACKUP VAULT BACKUP-properties set \

—name recoveryvault \

—resource-group rg-dr \

—backup-storage-redundancy GeoRedundant

Replication Settings

• **Replication Frequency**: Every 30 seconds, 5 minutes, or 15 minutes

• **Recovery Point Retention**: 1–24 hours (short-term), 7–30 days (long-term)

• **Crash-Consistent vs App-Consistent**: Use app-aware snapshots for SQL/Exchange

Failover and Failback Operations

Types of Failover:

• **Test Failover**: Validate recovery plan without disrupting production

• **Planned Failover**: Controlled switchover with no data loss

- **Unplanned Failover**: Triggered during disaster; may lose in-flight data

Failback is available from Azure to on-prem (after DR event ends).

CLI Example for Test Failover:

az backup recoverypoint list \

—vault-name recoveryvault \

—resource-group rg-dr \

—container-name vm01 \

—item-name vm01

Designing Recovery Plans

RECOVERY PLANS DEFINE:

- Boot order of VMs
- Dependencies (e.g., DB before App Server)
- Scripts or Azure Automation for custom actions
- Manual approvals or alerts

Best Practices:

- Use a separate plan for each environment or workload group
- Include **pre/post failover scripts** for DNS, load balancer reconfiguration
- Schedule regular **test failovers**

Monitoring and Compliance

USE **Azure Monitor** and **Backup Center** for centralized visibility:

- Backup job status
- Vault usage and costs
- Alerting on failed or incomplete jobs

Recommended Alerts:

- Backup job failed
- Recovery point expired
- Replication health degraded

KQL Sample:

```
AzureDiagnostics
| where Category == "AzureBackupReport"
| where Status_s != "Completed"
| summarize count() by Resource, ResultType_s
```

Security and Retention Compliance

- **Encrypt backups** with Microsoft or Customer Managed Keys
- **Soft Delete** enabled by default (14-day undelete window)
- **Immutable Vaults**: Protect from ransomware or internal threats
- **RBAC**: Define roles for backup operator, restore-only user, etc.

Cost Considerations

AZURE BACKUP AND SITE Recovery are priced based on:

- **Instance Size**
- **Retention Duration**
- **Storage Type (LRS vs GRS)**
- **Replication Frequency and Failover Readiness**

Tips:

- Use **Cool Blob Tier** for long-term backup storage
- Archive infrequent restore points
- Avoid backing up transient dev/test workloads unless needed

---

Testing Your DR Strategy

- **Quarterly failover drills** for each application
- Simulate region unavailability
- Use **Chaos Studio** for failure injection
- Track RPO/RTO adherence metrics

Documentation Should Include:

- Recovery Runbooks
- DR Communication Plans
- Compliance Mapping (ISO, HIPAA, etc.)

Summary

AZURE BACKUP AND SITE Recovery provide the foundation for a comprehensive data protection and disaster recovery plan. With flexible backup policies, zone and region-aware replication, automation support, and detailed monitoring capabilities, these services help you ensure continuity even under adverse conditions.

Architectural Takeaways:

- Use **Recovery Services Vaults** to centralize protection
- Define clear **backup policies** with tiered retention
- Deploy **Site Recovery** to protect critical workloads across regions
- Create **Recovery Plans** with orchestration and automation
- Monitor job health and enforce compliance via alerts and audit logs
- Regularly **test your DR strategy** and refine based on results

In the next section, we will scale our resilience strategy to multi-region architectures, focusing on design patterns for active-active, active-passive, and cross-zone deployments across Azure's global network.

Designing Multi-Region and Cross-Zone Deployments

DESIGNING CLOUD SOLUTIONS to span across availability zones and regions is essential for achieving true resiliency, low-latency performance, and business continuity. While zone-level resilience protects against datacenter failures within a region, **multi-region architecture** ensures operational continuity even if an entire Azure region becomes unavailable due to disaster, geopolitical disruption, or large-scale maintenance.

This section explores the design principles, architectural patterns, Azure-native services, automation strategies, and trade-offs involved in implementing cross-zone and multi-region solutions. You'll learn how to deploy highly available, geographically resilient applications with seamless failover, optimized performance, and compliance-ready configurations.

Azure Global Infrastructure Overview

AZURE'S GLOBAL INFRASTRUCTURE spans over 60+ regions and includes **Availability Zones, Paired Regions**, and **Edge Locations**. These components form the foundation for architecting regional and cross-zone redundancy.

Availability Zones

- INDEPENDENT DATACENTERS within a region
- Each with its own power, cooling, and network
- Guarantees 99.99% uptime when used properly

Region Pairs

- EACH AZURE REGION is paired with another in the same geography
- Data replication and service updates are coordinated
- Provides foundational support for disaster recovery and compliance

Edge Zones

- BRING COMPUTE AND storage closer to users
- Used to reduce latency for IoT, gaming, and real-time apps

Design Objectives for Cross-Zone and Multi-Region Deployments

1. **High Availability**: Minimize downtime across any failure domain.
2. **Fault Isolation**: Prevent failure from cascading across services or regions.
3. **Performance Optimization**: Serve content closer to users using global distribution.
4. **Disaster Recovery**: Ensure operational continuity in the event of catastrophic outages.
5. **Compliance Alignment**: Fulfill geographic and regulatory constraints.

Key Patterns and Architectures

Active-Active Multi-Region

- DEPLOY FULL INSTANCES of an application in two or more Azure regions.
- Traffic is distributed based on proximity, availability, or load.
- Requires stateless app design or cross-region session replication.

Use Case: Global web applications, financial systems with low RTO/RPO, e-commerce platforms.

Active-Passive with Cold or Warm Standby

- PRIMARY REGION SERVES all traffic; secondary region remains on standby.
- DR region may have infrastructure deployed but scaled down (warm) or provisioned on demand (cold).
- DNS or Front Door handles redirection during failover.

Use Case: Enterprise systems with moderate SLA requirements, ERP systems.

Zone-Redundant within a Region

- APPLICATION TIERS deployed across availability zones within a single region.
- Load balanced across zones using Azure Load Balancer or Application Gateway.

Use Case: Applications that must meet 99.99% uptime without geographic distribution.

Azure Services and Cross-Zone/Region Resiliency

Azure Service	Zone Redundant	Multi-Region Capability
Azure Load Balancer	Yes	No (region-scoped)
Azure Front Door	N/A	Yes (global entry point)
Azure App Service	Yes	Manual regional deployment
Azure Kubernetes Service	Yes	Multi-cluster design per region
Azure SQL Database	Yes (ZRS)	Auto-failover groups, geo-replication
Azure Storage	ZRS, GZRS	RA-GRS, GZRS
Azure Cosmos DB	Yes	Multi-region writes and failover

Traffic Management Across Regions

Azure Front Door

- LAYER 7 GLOBAL LOAD balancer and CDN
- Intelligent health probing and automatic failover
- SSL offload and URL routing

Example Scenario: Route 70% of traffic to West Europe and 30% to North Europe for load distribution.

Azure Traffic Manager

- DNS-BASED ROUTING with priority, performance, or geographic methods

- Slower failover due to DNS TTL (~30 seconds or more)

Priority Routing Example:

az network traffic-manager profile create \

—name my-traffic \

—resource-group rg-global \

—routing-method Priority \

—unique-dns-name my-global-app \

—ttl 30 \

—monitor-path /health

Application Architecture Considerations

Stateless Design

- APPLICATIONS SHOULD not rely on server affinity.
- Use distributed caches like Azure Cache for Redis.

State Synchronization

- FOR SESSION DATA, use geo-replicated storage (e.g., Cosmos DB, Azure SQL).
- Enable cross-region data writes with conflict resolution logic.

Data Gravity Mitigation

- MINIMIZE CROSS-REGION data access to reduce latency.

• Co-locate compute with data wherever possible.

Storage and Database Strategies

Azure Storage

• USE **ZRS** for zone redundancy within a region.

• Use **GZRS** or **RA-GZRS** for cross-region redundancy.

Azure SQL Database

• CONFIGURE **Auto-Failover Groups** between regions.

• Built-in replication with RPO < 5 seconds and failover automation.

```
az sql failover-group create \
—name failovergroup1 \
—partner-server sql-secondary \
—resource-group rg-db \
—server sql-primary \
—failover-policy Automatic
```

Cosmos DB

• SUPPORT FOR **multi-region writes**

• Manual or automatic failover

• Five consistency levels to balance performance and availability

Automation and Infrastructure as Code

AUTOMATE MULTI-REGION deployment using:

- **ARM Templates**
- **Bicep**
- **Terraform**
- **Azure DevOps Pipelines**

Example: Bicep for Regional Deployment

```
resource webappPrimary 'Microsoft.Web/sites@2022-09-01' = {
name: 'myapp-we'
location: 'westeurope'
properties: {
serverFarmId: appServicePlan.id
}
}
resource webappSecondary 'Microsoft.Web/sites@2022-09-01' = {
name: 'myapp-ne'
location: 'northeurope'
properties: {
serverFarmId: appServicePlan.id
}
```

```
}
```

Observability and Monitoring

ENABLE OBSERVABILITY for cross-region solutions:

- Use **Azure Monitor** and **Log Analytics** to track availability and latency.
- Configure health probes for all load balancers and routing services.
- Integrate with **Application Insights** for distributed tracing across regions.

KQL Example:

```
requests
| where cloud_RoleName == "myapp-we"
| summarize avg(duration) by bin(timestamp, 5m)
```

Testing Multi-Region Resiliency

REGULARLY VALIDATE failover capabilities:

- Perform **Test Failovers** in DR regions
- Use **Azure Chaos Studio** to simulate region outages
- Validate **DNS propagation time**, **session continuity**, and **data consistency**
- Track **RTO and RPO** metrics during failover events

Test Plan Components:

- Pre-failover snapshot and baseline validation
- Automated script to trigger DNS switch
- Post-failover recovery verification
- Metrics collection and SLA compliance audit

Compliance and Data Residency

MANY INDUSTRIES HAVE regulations requiring data to remain within geographic boundaries.

Approaches:

- Use **Azure Region Pairs** within same geography
- Avoid data replication to foreign jurisdictions
- Leverage **Customer Managed Keys** and **Private Endpoints** to enforce control

---

Cost Management and Optimization

MULTI-REGION DEPLOYMENTS introduce cost considerations:

- Compute duplication
- Storage replication
- Cross-region data egress

Optimization Tips:

- Use **Hot/Warm/Cold DR models** depending on workload criticality

- Leverage **reserved instances** in secondary regions
- Use **auto-scaling** in active-active scenarios to right-size compute
- Evaluate traffic distribution via **Azure Cost Management** reports

Summary

DESIGNING MULTI-REGION and cross-zone deployments is essential for creating resilient, scalable, and globally accessible Azure applications. By distributing resources across fault boundaries, leveraging Azure-native routing and replication tools, and aligning designs with RTO/RPO requirements, architects can deliver platforms that withstand major outages and deliver consistent user experiences.

Key Takeaways for Architects:

- Deploy across **zones and regions** to mitigate failures at any level
- Choose between **active-active** and **active-passive** models based on SLA
- Leverage **Azure Front Door**, **Traffic Manager**, and **GZRS** for availability
- Automate deployments and validate recovery plans frequently
- Monitor and optimize for **performance, compliance, and cost**

In the next section, we'll examine how to tailor business continuity designs for **mission-critical applications**, including zero-downtime strategies, compliance-heavy workloads, and complex multi-tiered solutions.

Business Continuity for Mission-Critical

Applications

MISSION-CRITICAL APPLICATIONS are those whose failure would cause significant disruption to business operations, financial loss, regulatory non-compliance, or reputational damage. These applications require the highest level of resilience, availability, and disaster recovery planning. In the Azure ecosystem, ensuring business continuity for such systems demands a comprehensive approach—one that blends high availability, fault tolerance, geo-redundancy, data integrity, compliance alignment, and automated failover.

This section provides an in-depth guide to architecting business continuity for mission-critical workloads. It covers architectural patterns, platform services, real-world examples, resilience testing, monitoring, and governance practices to ensure these workloads meet strict Recovery Time Objectives (RTO) and Recovery Point Objectives (RPO).

Characteristics of Mission-Critical Applications

MISSION-CRITICAL SYSTEMS vary by industry, but generally include:

- **Financial platforms** (e.g., banking, trading, payment gateways)
- **Healthcare systems** (e.g., EHR, telemedicine platforms)
- **Retail systems** (e.g., POS, inventory control)
- **Manufacturing control systems**
- **Government and defense workloads**
- **High-profile web platforms and SaaS apps**

Key requirements for such applications typically include:

- Near-zero **RTO/RPO**
- Regulatory compliance (HIPAA, PCI-DSS, ISO 27001)
- Data sovereignty and residency
- Real-time monitoring and observability
- Secure, auditable failover mechanisms
- End-to-end automation

Architectural Design Principles

1. **Fault Isolation and Redundancy**
   Segment workloads across zones, regions, and services to eliminate single points of failure.
2. **Stateless and Loosely Coupled Design**
   Services must restart independently and recover gracefully using load balancers and queues.
3. **Multi-Tiered Deployment**
   Decouple frontend, backend, and data services. Replicate and scale each tier independently.
4. **Geo-Redundancy**
   Active-active or active-passive deployments across Azure paired regions for seamless failover.
5. **Consistent Configuration**
   Use infrastructure as code (IaC) to maintain consistent environments in both primary and secondary regions.
6. **Monitoring and Automated Recovery**
   Deploy deep observability and use tools like Azure Monitor, Log Analytics, and Application Insights.

Resilient Azure Services for Mission-Critical Applications

Layer	Azure Service(s)	High Availability Features
Compute	Azure Kubernetes Service (AKS), App Service, VMs	Zonal deployment, auto-scaling, self-healing
Networking	Azure Front Door, Traffic Manager, App Gateway	Geo-routing, health probes, SSL offload
Storage	Azure Storage (GZRS/RA-GZRS), Azure Files, Azure NetApp	Zone and geo-redundant options
Data	Azure SQL Database, Cosmos DB, Azure PostgreSQL	Auto-failover, replication, multi-region writes
Identity	Azure AD, Conditional Access	Redundant auth endpoints, federation, seamless SSO
Observability	Azure Monitor, Application Insights, Log Analytics	End-to-end tracing and anomaly detection

Pattern: Active-Active with Global Load Distribution

USE CASE: A real-time financial trading app with zero tolerance for downtime.

Key Components:

- Two full Azure deployments in West Europe and North Europe.
- Azure Front Door with round-robin or performance-based routing.

- Cosmos DB with multi-region writes and session-level consistency.
- Azure SQL Database configured with auto-failover group.
- Blob storage with GZRS and versioning enabled.
- Azure Key Vault with geo-redundant secrets.

Benefits:

- Immediate availability during regional failure.
- Load distribution based on geographic location.
- Minimal-to-zero RPO and RTO.

Pattern: Active-Passive with Hot Standby

USE CASE: A core HR/payroll system with strict compliance requirements.

Key Components:

- Primary region handles all traffic.
- Secondary region provisioned with infrastructure, kept in sync.
- Data replication using SQL auto-failover groups and RA-GRS storage.
- Azure Traffic Manager configured with priority routing.

Failover Flow:

1. Azure Monitor detects outage.
2. Traffic Manager routes to passive region.
3. Automated scripts restore frontends from templates if

necessary.
4. DNS TTLs expire and users reroute to new region.
5. Health probes validate restoration.

Recovery Time Goal: < 15 minutes

Data Strategy for Mission-Critical Workloads

SQL Databases

- USE **Auto-Failover Groups** for cross-region recovery.
- Combine with **Geo-Replication** and point-in-time restore.

Cosmos DB

- ENABLE **multi-region writes.**
- Choose appropriate **consistency model** (session/strong/eventual).
- Monitor **replication lag** and failover health.

Storage

- SELECT **GZRS** for storage accounts.
- Enable **soft delete** and **immutable blob storage** for compliance.
- Use **Azure Backup Vaults** with long-term retention policies.

Secrets Management

- USE **Azure Key Vault Premium** with geo-redundancy.

• Periodically back up secrets and use RBAC to control access.

Security and Compliance Requirements

MISSION-CRITICAL SYSTEMS are often governed by:

• **GDPR**: Ensure data residency and subject rights.

• **HIPAA**: Enforce encryption, audit logs, and business associate agreements.

• **PCI-DSS**: Secure cardholder data and apply strict access controls.

• **ISO/IEC 27001**: Implement ISMS-aligned controls.

• **FedRAMP** (for US Gov): Follow authorized cloud baseline configurations.

Implementation Guidelines:

• Encrypt data at rest with **customer-managed keys (CMK)**.

• Use **Private Endpoints** to prevent public network exposure.

• Enable **Azure Defender for Cloud** for posture management.

• Audit access with **Azure Policy**, **Log Analytics**, and **Azure AD Sign-In Logs**.

Testing and Simulation

MISSION-CRITICAL DR strategies must be tested rigorously and frequently.

Test Types:

• **Planned Failovers**: Manually initiated for validation.

- **Unplanned Failovers**: Simulate disaster without advance warning.
- **Load Testing**: Validate scale and performance during regional spike.
- **Chaos Testing**: Use Azure Chaos Studio to test fault tolerance.

Metrics to Track:

- RTO and RPO adherence
- MTTR (Mean Time To Recovery)
- Data loss, transaction replay gaps
- Failover automation completeness
- SLA vs actual uptime variance

Observability and Alerting

MONITORING IS NON-NEGOTIABLE for mission-critical apps.

- Use **Application Insights** to trace transaction flows.
- Integrate **Log Analytics** with custom KQL dashboards.
- Configure **Azure Monitor Alerts** for:
    - SLA breaches
    - Dependency failures
    - Latency thresholds
    - Authentication issues

○ Health probe status from Front Door or Traffic Manager

Sample KQL Query:

```
availabilityResults
| where success == false
| summarize count() by bin(timestamp, 5m), location
```

Governance and Runbook Automation

ENSURE FAILOVER STEPS are documented and executable by automation tools:

- Use **Azure Automation**, **Logic Apps**, or **PowerShell Runbooks.**
- Include:
    - DNS switch procedures
    - Service restarts
    - Alert and notification system updates
    - Rollback steps (in case of failback)

Governance Artifacts:

- Business Continuity Plan (BCP)
- Disaster Recovery Plan (DRP)
- Application topology maps
- RACI matrix for failover roles

- Compliance audit logs and review cadence

Cost Implications

DESIGNING FOR 99.999% uptime and zero RPO is expensive.

Cost Driver	Description	Mitigation
Dual-region deployments	Compute, storage, and network duplication	Use reserved instances, scale down standby
Replication bandwidth	Cross-region egress for syncing data	Use compression, delta-only transfers
Premium services	Front Door, Premium Key Vault, Cosmos DB	Scale only critical workloads
License duplication	Windows, SQL, third-party licensing	Use Azure Hybrid Benefit where applicable

Summary

MISSION-CRITICAL APPLICATIONS demand best-in-class business continuity strategies that go beyond standard redundancy and recovery. By integrating multi-region infrastructure, intelligent traffic routing, highly available services, secure data replication, and resilient automation, architects can deliver platforms that meet the most demanding availability and compliance requirements.

Architectural Checklist:

- Design with **zone and region fault domains** in mind
- Ensure **near-zero RTO/RPO** through replication and automation
- Secure data using **geo-redundant**, **immutable**, and **encrypted** storage

- Validate designs using **failover tests**, **chaos engineering**, and **auditing**
- Document and automate all critical recovery workflows
- Monitor with deep observability and trigger real-time alerts

The next chapter will focus on designing core infrastructure—networking, compute, and hybrid connectivity—that supports the high-availability and business continuity strategies introduced here.

Chapter 5: Designing Infrastructure Solutions

Designing Virtual Networks and Subnetting

A WELL-ARCHITECTED Azure infrastructure begins with a strong foundation of networking. Virtual networks (VNets) in Azure serve as the backbone of secure, scalable, and performant solutions. VNets enable Azure resources to communicate with each other, with on-premises environments, and with the public internet. Subnetting, address planning, route tables, network security groups, and integration with other networking components such as DNS, firewalls, and private endpoints play a crucial role in any enterprise-grade architecture.

In this section, we'll explore how to design robust virtual network topologies, implement subnetting strategies, enforce segmentation, plan IP address allocation, integrate DNS and custom routing, and adhere to best practices for enterprise-scale deployments.

Understanding Azure Virtual Networks

AN AZURE VIRTUAL NETWORK (VNet) is a private, logically isolated network in the Azure cloud. It provides the same functionalities of a traditional on-premises network: IP addressing, name resolution, routing, access control, and connectivity to the internet and other networks.

Key Features of VNets:

- Define address spaces using private IP ranges (RFC 1918)
- Create subnets to segment workloads

- Route traffic via system or custom route tables
- Secure communication using NSGs and Azure Firewall
- Peer VNets for resource-level communication
- Integrate with VPN Gateways or ExpressRoute for hybrid connectivity

---

IP Address and Subnet Planning

PROPER IP ADDRESS PLANNING is foundational to avoid address exhaustion, routing conflicts, or segmentation issues. Plan IP ranges that do not overlap with on-premises or other cloud networks.

Recommended Private IP Ranges (RFC 1918):

- 10.0.0.0/8
- 172.16.0.0/12
- 192.168.0.0/16

Example VNet Address Space:

```
VNet CIDR: 10.0.0.0/16
├── Subnet-frontend: 10.0.1.0/24
├── Subnet-backend: 10.0.2.0/24
└── Subnet-database: 10.0.3.0/24
```

Best Practices:

- Reserve the first and last IP in each subnet (used by Azure)

- Avoid small subnets (/29 or smaller) for production
- Use larger blocks for expansion and dynamic scaling
- Tag subnets based on environment or workload (e.g., env:prod)

Subnet Segmentation Strategy

SUBNETS LOGICALLY DIVIDE a VNet and isolate workloads to improve security and manageability. Each subnet should serve a specific role:

Subnet Name	**Purpose**
Frontend	Hosts public-facing services (Web Apps, Load Balancer frontends)
Backend	Application tier (AKS, App Services, Logic Apps)
Database	Azure SQL, PostgreSQL, Cosmos DB
Management	Bastion, Jumpbox, DevOps agents
Integration	Private Link, VPN Gateways, ExpressRoute

Security Tip: Apply **NSGs (Network Security Groups)** at the subnet level to enforce east-west and north-south traffic control.

Creating a VNet with Subnets via CLI

AZ NETWORK VNET CREATE \

—name corp-vnet \

—resource-group rg-network \

—address-prefix 10.10.0.0/16 \

—subnet-name frontend-subnet \

—subnet-prefix 10.10.1.0/24

az network vnet subnet create \

—vnet-name corp-vnet \

—name backend-subnet \

—resource-group rg-network \

—address-prefix 10.10.2.0/24

Route Table and Custom Routing

BY DEFAULT, AZURE USES system routes that allow intra-VNet communication and internet access via NAT for public IP-enabled services.

Custom Routes (User Defined Routes – UDRs):

Use UDRs when:

- Forcing traffic through a Network Virtual Appliance (NVA) or Azure Firewall
- Blocking internet access from specific subnets
- Routing specific prefixes to VPNs or ExpressRoute gateways

Sample Route Table:

Destination Prefix	Next Hop Type	Next Hop IP
0.0.0.0/0	Virtual Appliance	10.10.0.4
10.20.0.0/16	Virtual Network	—
192.168.1.0/24	Virtual Network Gateway	—

Integrating DNS in VNets

AZURE AUTOMATICALLY assigns an internal DNS IP (e.g., 168.63.129.16) for name resolution within a VNet. You can override this with custom DNS servers.

Use Cases for Custom DNS:

- On-prem DNS integration via VPN/ExpressRoute
- Private DNS zones for internal service discovery
- DNS filtering or logging

Setting DNS Servers via CLI:

```
az network vnet update \
—name corp-vnet \
—resource-group rg-network \
—dns-servers 10.0.0.4 10.0.0.5
```

Private Link and Endpoint Integration

PRIVATE LINK ALLOWS you to access Azure PaaS services (e.g., Azure SQL, Blob Storage, Key Vault) over private IPs within your VNet.

Benefits:

- Avoids public internet exposure
- Enforces strict network boundary
- Logs and audits access through NSGs and traffic monitoring

Best Practice: Place private endpoints in a dedicated **integration subnet** to segregate traffic and simplify policies.

VNet Peering and Global Connectivity

VNET PEERING CONNECTS two VNets for low-latency, high-bandwidth communication.

Key Facts:

- Peering is non-transitive: VNet1 ↔ VNet2; VNet2 ↔ VNet3 ≠ VNet1 ↔ VNet3
- Peered VNets must use non-overlapping address spaces
- You can peer across subscriptions and regions (Global VNet Peering)

Peering via CLI:

az network vnet peering create \

—name vnet1-to-vnet2 \

—resource-group rg1 \

—vnet-name vnet1 \

—remote-vnet vnet2-id \

—allow-vnet-access

Network Security Groups (NSGs)

NSGS PROVIDE RULE-BASED traffic filtering at the subnet or NIC level.

Example Inbound NSG Rules:

Priority	Source	Port	Protocol	Action
100	VirtualNetwork	443	TCP	Allow
200	Internet	80	TCP	Deny

Best Practices:

- Deny by default; explicitly allow required traffic
- Separate NSGs for app, DB, and frontend subnets
- Log traffic using **NSG Flow Logs** via Network Watcher

Integration with Azure Firewall

FOR CENTRALIZED TRAFFIC inspection and logging:

- Route outbound/inbound traffic via Azure Firewall
- Use **Threat Intelligence**, **FQDN filtering**, and **Application Rules**
- Enable **Forced Tunneling** with UDRs

Key Concepts:

- Firewall in hub VNet
- Spoke VNets peer with hub
- UDR routes all 0.0.0.0/0 traffic to firewall

Hub-and-Spoke Network Topology

THIS ENTERPRISE PATTERN centralizes connectivity and services.

- **Hub VNet**: Shared services, security appliances, DNS, VPN
- **Spoke VNets**: Application workloads per environment or business unit

Advantages:

- Simplified management
- Scalable and modular
- Isolated security domains
- Efficient hybrid connectivity

Monitoring and Observability

USE **Network Watcher** to monitor, diagnose, and visualize network flows.

Capabilities:

- Connection Troubleshooting
- IP Flow Verify

- NSG Diagnostics
- Packet Capture
- Topology Viewer

Enable Network Watcher via CLI:

az network watcher configure \

—locations uksouth \

—resource-group rg-network \

—enabled true

Best Practices Checklist

- PLAN IP ADDRESSING carefully to avoid conflicts
- Segment workloads using subnets and NSGs
- Enable service endpoints or private link for PaaS traffic
- Use UDRs and Azure Firewall for traffic control
- Implement hub-and-spoke topology for scale
- Automate deployment using Bicep or Terraform
- Monitor traffic flows and NSG rules with Network Watcher

Summary

DESIGNING VIRTUAL NETWORKS and subnetting in Azure requires careful planning, clear segmentation, secure access controls, and efficient routing. These foundational decisions significantly impact the scalability, manageability, and security of your cloud infrastructure.

Architectural Essentials:

- Structure your VNet and subnet layout based on workload tiers and security zones.
- Use NSGs and route tables to control traffic direction and flow.
- Plan for growth with a non-overlapping IP schema and scalable CIDR blocks.
- Centralize services like firewalls, DNS, and VPN in hub VNets.
- Monitor continuously to detect misconfigurations or bottlenecks early.

In the next section, we'll build upon this foundation by exploring how to secure your virtual networks with advanced firewalling, private connectivity, service endpoints, and zero-trust segmentation strategies.

Configuring Network Security and Private Connectivity

AS WORKLOADS SHIFT to the cloud, protecting communication between services and controlling how data flows becomes paramount. Azure provides a layered security model that allows you to implement robust network segmentation, enforce least privilege access, and restrict exposure to only required endpoints. Network security involves configuring firewalls, access rules, and routing paths. Private connectivity refers to enabling secure, isolated channels for Azure services and hybrid networks using private IP space.

In this section, we explore how to secure virtual networks in Azure using Network Security Groups (NSGs), Azure Firewall, Private Link, Service Endpoints, route tables, and network monitoring tools. We'll also examine zero-trust models and practical implementations of hybrid connectivity using VPN and ExpressRoute. These tools enable Azure architects to design safe and compliant environments, minimizing attack surface and preventing lateral movement.

Principles of Network Security in Azure

AZURE FOLLOWS A **zero-trust** networking model, which assumes that breaches are inevitable and that every request should be authenticated, authorized, and encrypted regardless of origin.

Key Principles:

- **Deny by default**: All inbound and outbound traffic is blocked unless explicitly allowed.
- **Microsegmentation**: Divide networks and subnets into tightly controlled domains.
- **Explicit allow rules**: Whitelist known sources, ports, and protocols.
- **Network boundary enforcement**: Use firewalls and private access for service-to-service communication.
- **Identity-aware access**: Leverage Azure AD and conditional access policies.

Network Security Groups (NSGs)

NSGS ARE THE PRIMARY mechanism for filtering network traffic to and from Azure resources.

Components:

- **Inbound and outbound rules**
- Applied at **subnet or NIC level**
- Stateless (response traffic must be explicitly allowed)

Example NSG Rule Set:

Priority	Name	Direction	Port	Protocol
100	AllowHTTP	Inbound	80	TCP
200	AllowHTTPS	Inbound	443	TCP
300	DenyAllInbound	Inbound	*	*

CLI EXAMPLE:

```
az network nsg rule create \
—resource-group rg-security \
—nsg-name web-nsg \
—name Allow-HTTPS \
—priority 100 \
—direction Inbound \
—protocol Tcp \
```

—source-address-prefixes Internet \

—destination-port-ranges 443 \

—access Allow

Best Practices:

- Apply NSGs at both subnet and NIC level for granularity.
- Use **Application Security Groups (ASGs)** to group workloads by role.
- Periodically audit NSG rules and logs for misconfigurations or overly permissive rules.

Azure Firewall

AZURE FIREWALL IS A stateful, fully managed, cloud-native network security service.

Capabilities:

- Layer 3–7 inspection
- Application and Network rules
- Threat intelligence filtering
- Centralized logging and alerting
- DNS proxy and FQDN filtering

Use Case Example:

- Route all outbound internet-bound traffic through Azure Firewall.

- Inspect outbound HTTP/HTTPS calls for malware or command-and-control traffic.

- Block access to non-approved destinations using FQDN rules.

Firewall Deployment Strategy:

- Place in a **hub VNet** in a hub-and-spoke architecture.

- Create **User Defined Routes (UDRs)** in spoke VNets to forward traffic to firewall.

CLI UDR Example:

```
az network route-table route create \
—resource-group rg-network \
—route-table-name route-table-fw \
—name fw-default \
—address-prefix 0.0.0.0/0 \
—next-hop-type VirtualAppliance \
—next-hop-ip-address 10.0.0.4
```

Application Security Groups (ASGs)

ASGS ALLOW YOU TO GROUP network interfaces based on application roles, reducing IP dependency in NSGs.

Benefits:

- Simplify rule management

- Support dynamic scaling

- Improve readability and intent of rules

Example:

Create an ASG for all backend VMs and apply an NSG rule that only allows inbound traffic from the frontend ASG.

Service Endpoints

SERVICE ENDPOINTS ALLOW Azure resources to communicate with PaaS services using Azure backbone network instead of public IPs.

Supported Services:

- Azure Storage
- Azure SQL Database
- Cosmos DB
- Azure Key Vault
- Azure App Configuration

Benefits:

- Improves security by limiting access to subnet IPs
- Reduces data exfiltration risks
- No need for public IPs on services

Enabling Example:

az network vnet subnet update \

—name app-subnet \

—vnet-name corp-vnet \

—resource-group rg-network \

—service-endpoints Microsoft.Storage

Private Link and Private Endpoints

PRIVATE LINK ALLOWS you to map PaaS resources to private IP addresses within your VNet.

Use Cases:

- Secure communication with Azure SQL, Blob Storage, Key Vault, etc.
- Meet regulatory or compliance requirements for network isolation
- Avoid data exfiltration over public IPs

Deployment Steps:

1. Enable private endpoint for a resource (e.g., Key Vault)
2. Assign IP from designated subnet
3. Create DNS mapping (privatelink.<service>.core.windows.net)

Example for Private Endpoint Creation:

az network private-endpoint create \

—name kv-pe \

—resource-group rg-network \

—vnet-name vnet-hub \

—subnet subnet-integration \

—private-connection-resource-id /subscriptions/.../keyvaults/mykv \

—group-id vault \

—connection-name kvConnection

Hybrid Connectivity Security

VPN Gateway

- IPSEC/IKE TUNNEL to on-premises
- Supports policy-based and route-based VPNs
- Enforce NSGs and UDRs to control on-prem to Azure flows

ExpressRoute

- PRIVATE, DEDICATED circuit to Azure over MPLS
- SLA-backed, high-throughput link
- Use **Network Virtual Appliance (NVA)** or **Azure Firewall** for inspection

Security Considerations:

- Isolate VPN and ExpressRoute traffic in dedicated subnets
- Monitor tunnel health and logs using Azure Monitor
- Apply RBAC and logging to gateway configuration changes

Zero Trust Networking in Azure

ZERO TRUST ENFORCES the principle: **never trust, always verify.**

Core Concepts:

- Microsegmentation: NSGs, ASGs, UDRs
- Network boundary: Azure Firewall, NVA
- Identity-aware access: Azure AD, Conditional Access
- Encryption in transit: TLS, IPsec
- Monitoring and threat detection: Azure Sentinel, Defender for Cloud

Zero Trust Network Flow:

1. Workload starts request
2. Authentication with Azure AD
3. Request checked against NSG, ASG, and UDR
4. Sent through Azure Firewall
5. Logged, monitored, and flagged if anomalous

Network Monitoring and Auditing

USE **Azure Monitor**, **Network Watcher**, and **Defender for Cloud** for visibility.

Network Watcher Capabilities:

- CONNECTION TROUBLESHOOT

- Packet capture
- NSG flow logs
- Topology viewer

Defender for Cloud:

- ALERTS ON INSECURE NSGs (e.g., open to 0.0.0.0/0)
- Adaptive network hardening recommendations
- Threat detection for virtual networks

KQL for Open NSG Rule Detection:

```
AzureDiagnostics

| where Category == "NetworkSecurityGroupRuleCounter"

| where RemoteIP_s == "0.0.0.0/0" and Direction_s == "Inbound" and Access_s == "Allow"
```

Best Practices for Network Security and Private Access

- USE **NSGs** and **ASGs** to define least privilege network access
- Route all internet-bound traffic through **Azure Firewall**
- Enable **Private Endpoints** for all PaaS access in production
- Use **Service Endpoints** for simpler, faster network isolation
- Regularly audit rules and logs for misconfigurations
- Deploy **monitoring agents** and set up alert rules

• Enforce **naming conventions**, tagging, and documentation

Summary

NETWORK SECURITY AND private connectivity are vital pillars of secure cloud infrastructure. With Azure's comprehensive toolset—including NSGs, ASGs, Azure Firewall, Private Link, and routing policies—you can design highly segmented, secure, and performant networks that protect against modern threats while enabling flexible connectivity.

Architectural Recommendations:

• Isolate application tiers using subnets and NSGs

• Enforce zero-trust policies using identity and traffic-aware filters

• Use Private Link and UDRs to eliminate public exposure of services

• Centralize traffic control and inspection via Azure Firewall

• Monitor continuously using Network Watcher and Defender for Cloud

• Integrate hybrid connectivity securely using VPN or ExpressRoute

In the next section, we'll explore how to select the right compute options—including virtual machines, App Services, and containers—to meet application scalability, availability, and operational goals.

Choosing the Right Compute Option: VMs, App Services, and Containers

SELECTING THE APPROPRIATE compute model is a foundational decision when architecting solutions on Microsoft Azure. Compute resources power the application logic and services that support business processes. In Azure, compute options include **Virtual Machines (VMs)**, **App Services**, and **Containers (via AKS, ACI, or App Service for Containers)**. Each option offers distinct trade-offs in terms of flexibility, control, scalability, deployment complexity, and operational overhead.

This section provides an in-depth analysis of when to choose which compute model, including architectural patterns, scalability features, deployment strategies, cost considerations, and security implications. By aligning compute decisions with application requirements, Azure architects can ensure that solutions are efficient, maintainable, and cost-effective.

Compute Model Overview

Compute Type	Description	Ideal For
Virtual Machines (VMs)	IaaS-based servers running Windows or Linux	Legacy apps, custom OS/software, full control
App Services	PaaS-hosted managed web apps and APIs	Web apps, REST APIs, low-maintenance apps
Containers	Containerized workloads via AKS, ACI, or App Service	Microservices, modern apps, orchestration

EACH MODEL SUPPORTS different levels of abstraction and management responsibility in the **Shared Responsibility Model**.

When to Use Azure Virtual Machines

AZURE VMS PROVIDE THE highest level of control over the operating system, networking, and software stack.

Use Cases:

- Lift-and-shift of legacy workloads
- Applications requiring custom OS configurations
- Services that need to run persistent background jobs or agents
- Hosting third-party software that is not cloud-native
- SAP, SQL Server with complex licensing/customization

Key Features:

- Supports Windows, Linux, and specialized images (e.g., GPU-optimized, confidential compute)
- Can be deployed in **availability sets**, **zones**, or **proximity placement groups**
- Managed via **Azure Arc** for hybrid governance

Example CLI:

```
az vm create \
—resource-group rg-compute \
—name appvm01 \
—image UbuntuLTS \
—size Standard_D2s_v3 \
```

—admin-username azureuser \

—generate-ssh-keys

Best Practices:

- Use **managed disks** with appropriate redundancy (Premium SSD, ZRS)
- Protect with **Azure Backup** and **Site Recovery**
- Integrate with **Azure Monitor** and **Log Analytics**
- Apply updates using **Azure Update Management**

Limitations:

- Manual scaling
- Higher operational overhead
- Slower provisioning compared to PaaS options

When to Use Azure App Services

AZURE APP SERVICES provide a fully managed PaaS environment for web applications, REST APIs, and mobile backends.

Use Cases:

- .NET, Java, Node.js, Python, PHP, or Ruby web applications
- CI/CD-enabled environments with zero-downtime deployments
- Multitenant SaaS platforms with per-customer app instances

- Applications requiring auto-scaling without infrastructure management

Key Features:

- Built-in **DevOps integration** (GitHub, Azure DevOps)
- **Deployment slots** for blue-green or canary deployments
- **Auto-scaling, custom domains**, and **SSL certificates**
- Supports **VNet integration**, **Private Endpoints**, and **Managed Identity**

App Service Plan Types:

Plan Type	Description
Free/Shared	Dev/test environments, limited usage
Basic/Standard	Production workloads, scaling support
PremiumV3	Enhanced performance, scaling, zone redundancy
Isolated (ASE)	VNet-integrated, fully private instances

CLI Example:

```
az webapp create \
—resource-group rg-app \
—plan myAppServicePlan \
—name mywebapp01 \
—runtime "NODE|18-lts"
```

Benefits:

- No infrastructure management

- Quick deployment and scaling
- Built-in security, logging, and diagnostic tools

Limitations:

- Less flexibility than VMs
- Not suitable for apps with OS-level dependencies
- Pricing can scale quickly with Premium tiers

When to Use Containers

CONTAINER-BASED COMPUTE enables consistent, isolated, and portable environments. Azure offers multiple services for running containers:

1. Azure Kubernetes Service (AKS)

AKS IS A FULLY MANAGED Kubernetes orchestration service.

Use Cases:

- Microservice applications
- CI/CD-driven workloads
- Horizontal scaling and self-healing deployments
- Apps requiring Helm, Istio, or custom Kubernetes controllers

Features:

- Cluster auto-scaling and node pools
- Integration with Azure DevOps, GitHub Actions

- Persistent storage using Azure Disks or Azure Files
- Secure container registries (ACR) and private clusters

```
az aks create \
—resource-group rg-k8s \
—name myCluster \
—node-count 3 \
—enable-addons monitoring \
—generate-ssh-keys
```

2. Azure Container Instances (ACI)

ACI PROVIDES SERVERLESS containers for short-lived or bursty workloads.

Use Cases:

- Job processing or scheduled tasks
- Lightweight APIs or cron-like workloads
- Dev/test containers

```
az container create \
—resource-group rg-container \
—name myapp \
—image myacr.azurecr.io/webapi:latest \
—cpu 1 \
```

—memory 1.5 \

—registry-login-server myacr.azurecr.io \

—ip-address Public

3. App Service for Containers

RUN DOCKER CONTAINERS inside App Service.

Use Cases:

- Containerized apps with minimal orchestration needs
- Hybrid PaaS–CaaS scenarios

az webapp create \

—resource-group rg-app \

—plan myAppServicePlan \

—name mycontainerapp \

—deployment-container-image-name myacr.azurecr.io/myapp:latest

Best Practices for Container Workloads:

- Use **Azure Container Registry (ACR)** for secure image storage
- Automate deployments using **GitHub Actions** or **Azure DevOps**
- Enforce **resource limits** and **pod security policies**
- Implement **CI/CD gates, linting,** and **vulnerability scans**

Comparative Decision Matrix

Criteria	Virtual Machines	App Services	Containers (AKS/ ACI)
OS-Level Control	Full	Limited	Moderate (depends on base image)
Startup Time	Slow (minutes)	Fast (seconds)	Fast (seconds)
Scaling	Manual / VMSS	Auto-scaling supported	Horizontal pod autoscaling
Managed by Azure	Partial	Fully	Partial (AKS), Full (ACI)
Deployment Complexity	High	Low	Medium (AKS), Low (ACI)
Use Case	Legacy, Stateful apps	Web apps, APIs	Microservices, batch, hybrid

Cost Considerations

- **App Services** tend to be cost-effective for small to medium workloads.
- **VMs** offer price-performance for compute-heavy or license-optimized scenarios (e.g., with Hybrid Benefit).
- **AKS** introduces some operational overhead but scales efficiently.
- **ACI** is billed per second and ideal for bursty workloads.

Use **Azure Pricing Calculator** and **Cost Management + Billing** to evaluate and monitor compute costs.

Security and Governance

REGARDLESS OF COMPUTE model:

- Apply **Managed Identity** for secure Azure resource access.
- Use **Defender for Cloud** to monitor vulnerabilities and security posture.
- Set **RBAC** policies on App Services and container registries.
- Enforce **image scanning** and **code signing** for containers.
- Use **private networking** (VNet Integration, Private Endpoints) for secure communication.

Monitoring and Observability

USE **Azure Monitor**, **Log Analytics**, and **Application Insights** to track performance and reliability.

- **VMs**: Install monitoring agents, collect OS metrics and logs.
- **App Services**: Enable Application Insights and Diagnostic Logs.
- **AKS**: Use Container Insights, Prometheus, and custom dashboards.
- **ACI**: Logs available via Azure Monitor and diagnostic settings.

Sample KQL Query for App Insights:

```
requests
| where cloud_RoleName == "myapp"
| summarize avg(duration) by bin(timestamp, 5m)
```

Summary

CHOOSING THE RIGHT Azure compute model requires aligning your technical, operational, and business requirements with the strengths of VMs, App Services, and containers. Each has distinct advantages depending on your need for control, scalability, performance, and deployment complexity.

Architectural Guidelines:

- Use **VMs** for legacy or highly customized workloads.
- Use **App Services** for web apps and APIs that benefit from PaaS.
- Use **Containers (AKS/ACI)** for microservices and DevOps-oriented architectures.
- Automate deployments and enforce security using CI/CD pipelines and policy controls.
- Monitor performance, cost, and security posture continuously.

In the next section, we'll focus on designing scalable and elastic compute solutions that dynamically adapt to workload demand while ensuring optimal cost and performance balance.

Architecting Scalable and Elastic Solutions

SCALABILITY AND ELASTICITY are critical pillars of cloud-native architecture. Applications must scale efficiently to handle varying load patterns, seasonal traffic spikes, and unpredictable growth—while maintaining performance, availability, and cost control. Azure provides a wide array of tools, services, and design patterns that allow architects to build scalable systems that can grow or shrink on demand, automatically adapt to usage, and maintain service-level objectives across distributed environments.

In this section, we'll explore the concepts and architectural strategies for building scalable and elastic solutions on Azure. Topics include horizontal and vertical scaling, scale units and statelessness, autoscaling, asynchronous messaging, distributed caching, event-driven architecture, and patterns for resiliency under load.

Scalability vs Elasticity

Concept	Definition
Scalability	The ability of a system to increase (or decrease) resources to handle load
Elasticity	The degree to which a system can automatically scale up/down as needed

SCALABILITY CAN BE **vertical** (scale-up) or **horizontal** (scale-out), whereas elasticity is usually horizontal and dynamic.

Goal: Architect systems that **scale-out** predictably and **elasticity** responds automatically to workload changes.

Azure Scaling Mechanisms

AZURE OFFERS BUILT-in scaling features across compute, data, and application services.

Resource Type	Scaling Method	Service/Feature
Virtual Machines	Manual / Autoscale	VM Scale Sets
App Services	Auto / Scheduled	App Service Plans
AKS (Containers)	Horizontal Pod Autoscaler	Kubernetes Scaling Policies
Azure SQL DB	vCore or DTU scaling	Auto-scale, Hyperscale tier
Cosmos DB	Request Units (RU/s)	Auto-scaling throughput
Storage Accounts	Managed (Azure handles)	Auto-scale with usage

Designing Horizontally Scalable Applications

HORIZONTAL SCALING involves adding more instances to distribute workload.

Architectural Considerations:

- Design **stateless services**: Store state in Redis, Azure Blob, or databases
- Use **load balancers** (Application Gateway, Azure Front Door) to distribute traffic
- Automate scaling rules based on performance counters (CPU, memory, queue length)
- Decouple services with **queues**, **event grids**, and **service buses**

Example: App Service Autoscaling Rule (CLI):

az monitor autoscale create \

—resource-group rg-app \

```
—resource myappservice \
—resource-type Microsoft.Web/sites \
—name autoscale-web \
—min-count 2 \
—max-count 10 \
—count 2
az monitor autoscale rule create \
—resource-group rg-app \
—autoscale-name autoscale-web \
—condition "CpuPercentage > 70 avg 5m" \
—scale out 1
```

Vertical Scaling (Scale-Up)

VERTICAL SCALING increases capacity (CPU, memory, IOPS) of a single resource.

When to use:

- Scaling database instances (e.g., move from GP_S_Gen5_2 to Gen5_8)
- Performance tuning for memory/CPU-bound workloads
- Situations where horizontal scaling is not feasible (e.g., monolithic apps)

Limitations:

- Downtime may be required
- Upper-bound on maximum size
- Not resilient to hardware failure like horizontal scaling

Statelessness and Scale Units

STATELESSNESS is critical for scale-out architecture. No request should rely on data held in memory or disk on a specific instance.

Strategies:

- Use **Azure Cache for Redis** for session storage
- Store uploaded files in **Azure Blob Storage**
- Authenticate using **JWT** or **OAuth 2.0** tokens (token-based auth)
- Partition resources into **scale units**—functional or tenant-based isolation

Scale Unit Example:

- Frontend Tier → Load Balancer → App Service
- Middleware Tier → Logic Apps or Azure Functions
- Data Tier → Azure SQL Hyperscale or Cosmos DB

Autoscaling Compute Resources

AZURE PROVIDES SEVERAL autoscaling mechanisms:

Azure App Service Autoscaling

- BASED ON METRICS like CPU, memory, HTTP queue length

- Schedule-based rules (e.g., weekend scale-in)

Azure Virtual Machine Scale Sets (VMSS)

- AUTOMATICALLY ADDS/removes VM instances
- Supports **custom image**, **ephemeral disks**, and **zonal deployment**

```
az vmss create \
—resource-group rg-compute \
—name myScaleSet \
—image UbuntuLTS \
—upgrade-policy-mode automatic \
—admin-username azureuser \
—generate-ssh-keys \
—vm-sku Standard_B2s \
—instance-count 2
```

Azure Kubernetes Service (AKS)

- HORIZONTAL POD AUTOSCALER (HPA): Scales pods based on CPU or custom metrics
- Cluster Autoscaler: Scales nodes in/out as needed

Example: HPA YAML

```
apiVersion: autoscaling/v1
```

kind: HorizontalPodAutoscaler

metadata:

name: webapp-hpa

spec:

maxReplicas: 10

minReplicas: 2

targetCPUUtilizationPercentage: 70

scaleTargetRef:

apiVersion: apps/v1

kind: Deployment

name: webapp

Messaging and Asynchronous Workflows

TO REDUCE TIGHT COUPLING and improve scalability, use asynchronous messaging.

Key Services:

Service	Description
Azure Service Bus	Enterprise-grade pub-sub and queueing
Azure Event Grid	Event routing for serverless workflows
Azure Queue	Lightweight queueing for storage tasks
Event Hubs	Stream ingestion for analytics pipelines

Benefits:

- Buffer traffic during spikes

- Decouple producers and consumers
- Add retry, dead-letter, and priority handling

Best Practices:

- Use **message batching** and **prefetch** to optimize throughput
- Scale consumers based on **queue depth metrics**
- Apply **dead-letter queues** for failed messages

Caching for Scalability

CACHING ENHANCES PERFORMANCE by reducing redundant computation and lowering backend load.

Common Use Cases:

- Session storage
- Frequently accessed data
- Database query results
- API response caching

Tools:

- **Azure Cache for Redis**
- **Content Delivery Network (CDN)** for static assets
- **Application Gateway and Front Door** for response caching

Example: Azure Redis CLI

```
az redis create \
```

—name mycache \

—resource-group rg-app \

—location uksouth \

—sku Premium \

—vm-size P1

Resiliency Patterns Under Load

HIGH-TRAFFIC SCENARIOS demand systems that not only scale but degrade gracefully.

Key Patterns:

- **Circuit Breaker**: Prevent repeated failures
- **Retry with Exponential Backoff**: Handle transient errors
- **Bulkhead**: Isolate failures across service domains
- **Queue-Based Load Leveling**: Buffer requests during spikes
- **Throttling and Rate Limiting**: Protect backend services

Azure Tools for Resiliency:

- API Management: Rate limiting, caching, and throttling
- Azure Front Door: Health probes and traffic shaping
- Application Gateway: Connection draining, WAF, and URL routing

---

Monitoring and Autoscale Tuning

TO EFFECTIVELY SCALE, observability is essential.

Metrics to Monitor:

- CPU usage
- Memory utilization
- HTTP request rate and response time
- Queue length (Service Bus, Storage Queue)
- RU consumption (Cosmos DB)
- Custom business metrics (e.g., order volume)

KQL Example:

```
AzureMetrics
| where Resource == "mywebapp" and MetricName == "CpuPercentage"
| summarize avg(Total) by bin(TimeGenerated, 5m)
```

Alerting:

- Set alerts for threshold breaches (e.g., CPU > 80%)
- Integrate alerts with Azure Automation or Logic Apps for autoscale triggers

---

Cost Optimization

SCALING INCREASES COST. Elasticity aims to reduce cost during low demand.

Strategies:

- Use **scheduled scaling** for predictable load
- Scale to zero (with Functions, ACI) during idle periods
- Use **spot VMs** or **reserved instances** for predictable workloads
- Apply **budgets** and **alerts** in Azure Cost Management

Summary

ARCHITECTING SCALABLE and elastic solutions ensures applications remain performant, available, and cost-effective under dynamic workloads. Azure provides a powerful suite of tools—from autoscaling compute resources to message-based decoupling and cache layers—that support modern, cloud-native design.

Architectural Guidelines:

- Design for horizontal scale first, vertical scale second
- Use autoscaling rules with clear metrics and guardrails
- Offload state, assets, and metadata to centralized services
- Employ asynchronous messaging to improve system throughput
- Cache frequently accessed data to reduce backend pressure
- Implement resiliency patterns and monitor aggressively
- Regularly test scaling behavior under simulated load

In the next section, we will examine hybrid network integration patterns using Azure ExpressRoute, VPN gateways, and private peering to seamlessly bridge on-premises and cloud environments.

Integrating Hybrid Networks with ExpressRoute and VPN Gateways

IN ENTERPRISE ENVIRONMENTS, full migration to the cloud is often not immediate or feasible. Many organizations operate in a **hybrid model**, where workloads are distributed across on-premises datacenters and cloud platforms. Ensuring seamless, secure, and performant network integration between Azure and on-premises infrastructure is crucial for maintaining business continuity, supporting legacy systems, meeting compliance mandates, and enabling gradual cloud adoption.

Azure provides two primary connectivity solutions for hybrid networks: **VPN Gateways** and **ExpressRoute**. Each serves different needs, with options for encryption, performance, cost, availability, and integration complexity.

In this section, we'll explore the architectures, deployment strategies, and best practices for integrating Azure with on-premises networks using VPN and ExpressRoute. We'll cover scenarios such as site-to-site VPNs, ExpressRoute circuits, private peering, BGP configuration, coexistence of VPN + ExpressRoute, failover strategies, and governance considerations.

Understanding Hybrid Connectivity Scenarios

Scenario	Description
Development/Test Connectivity	Use VPN gateway to connect to dev/test workloads in Azure
Production Hybrid Application	Use ExpressRoute for predictable latency and SLAs
Backup/DR Connectivity	Extend site-to-site VPN or ExpressRoute to Azure Recovery
Gradual Cloud Migration	Migrate workloads over ExpressRoute while maintaining hybrid
Secure SaaS Access	Route traffic to Microsoft SaaS (e.g., M365) over ExpressRoute

VPN Gateway: Overview and Use Cases

AZURE **VPN Gateway** enables encrypted IPsec/IKE connections between Azure VNets and on-premises locations.

Features:

- Route-based and policy-based VPNs
- Support for BGP routing
- Active-active configurations for high availability
- Point-to-site (P2S) and site-to-site (S2S) modes
- Integration with Virtual WAN for simplified large-scale connectivity

Use Cases:

- Fast setup for proof of concept or dev/test

- Temporary or low-bandwidth production needs
- Encrypted communications across the public internet

VPN Gateway Architecture

COMPONENTS:

- **Virtual Network Gateway**: Deployed in a dedicated gateway subnet
- **On-prem VPN device**: Physical or software device supporting IPsec/IKE
- **Gateway Subnet**: Subnet named GatewaySubnet with minimum /27 CIDR

Provisioning Example (CLI):

```
az network vnet create \

—name vnet-hybrid \

—resource-group rg-network \

—address-prefix 10.10.0.0/16 \

—subnet-name GatewaySubnet \

—subnet-prefix 10.10.255.0/27

az network public-ip create \

—resource-group rg-network \

—name vnetgw-pip

az network vnet-gateway create \
```

—name vnetgw \

—resource-group rg-network \

—vnet vnet-hybrid \

—public-ip-address vnetgw-pip \

—gateway-type Vpn \

—vpn-type RouteBased \

—sku VpnGw2 \

—no-wait

Configuration Notes:

- Ensure correct MTU settings (typically 1400 bytes)
- Define local network gateway with on-prem IP and prefixes
- Use pre-shared keys or certificate-based authentication

ExpressRoute: Overview and Enterprise Use Cases

AZURE EXPRESSROUTE provides private connectivity between Azure and on-premises networks via a dedicated line.

Key Features:

- Bypasses the public internet
- SLA-backed performance and uptime
- Integration with **Microsoft Peering** for M365 and Dynamics
- **Private Peering** for VNet traffic

- Redundant paths by default (dual links)

Use Cases:

- Mission-critical applications with low latency demands
- High-volume data transfer (e.g., replication, analytics)
- Regulatory compliance (e.g., PCI-DSS, HIPAA, ISO)
- Latency-sensitive applications (e.g., finance, real-time bidding)

ExpressRoute Architecture

Peering Type	Traffic Type
Private Peering	VNet-to-on-premises (private IP communication)
Microsoft Peering	Microsoft SaaS (e.g., M365, Power Platform)
Public Peering	Deprecated – legacy model

EXPRESSROUTE CIRCUIT Creation (Simplified CLI):

```
az network express-route create \
—name er-circuit \
—resource-group rg-network \
—bandwidth 200 \
—provider "BT" \
—peering-location "London" \
—sku-tier Premium \
—sku-family MeteredData
```

Gateway Configuration for VNet Integration:

az network vnet-gateway create \

—name er-vnet-gw \

—resource-group rg-network \

—vnet vnet-hybrid \

—gateway-type ExpressRoute \

—sku ErGw2AZ \

—location uksouth \

—public-ip-address er-vnetgw-pip

BGP Configuration and Routing

BORDER GATEWAY PROTOCOL (BGP) enables dynamic route advertisement between Azure and on-prem.

Advantages:

- Simplifies route management
- Prevents asymmetric routing
- Supports multiple on-prem and Azure prefixes

ExpressRoute BGP Peering Example:

- Configure ASN, peering IPs, and VLAN IDs on both sides
- Advertise internal IP prefixes using BGP communities

Common BGP ASN Ranges:

- Private ASN: 64512–65534
- Public ASN: Must be registered with regional internet registries

VPN and ExpressRoute Coexistence

AZURE SUPPORTS **VPN and ExpressRoute coexistence** for:

- **Failover Scenarios**: VPN as backup when ExpressRoute fails
- **Gradual Migration**: Transition from VPN to ExpressRoute over time
- **Split Routing**: Certain traffic over VPN, others over ExpressRoute

Coexistence Configuration:

- Use **same virtual network gateway**
- VPN Gateway must be deployed with **ErGw SKU**
- BGP routing ensures correct path selection and failover

High Availability and Redundancy

VPN GATEWAY HA:

- Active-active gateways with two public IPs
- Redundant on-prem VPN devices

ExpressRoute HA:

- Dual physical connections (required)
- Redundant Microsoft edge routers

- Integration with Azure Virtual WAN for large-scale architectures

Best Practices:

- Monitor tunnel health and failover readiness
- Use **Azure Monitor** and **Network Watcher**
- Regularly test failover scenarios (planned and unplanned)

Network Integration Patterns

Hub-and-Spoke with ExpressRoute

- HUB VNET HOSTS THE ExpressRoute gateway
- Spokes peer with hub for access to on-premises
- Centralized NSGs, firewalls, and route tables

Virtual WAN Integration

- SIMPLIFIES LARGE-scale, multi-region connectivity
- Automates route propagation and tunnel management
- Supports ExpressRoute and VPN simultaneously

VNet Peering Across Regions

- COMBINE EXPRESSROUTE in one region with peered VNets in others
- Use **Global VNet Peering** for non-transitive connectivity

Security and Compliance

- USE **Private Endpoints** for PaaS service access over ExpressRoute
- Apply **NSGs, route filters**, and **firewalls** for control
- Enable **diagnostic logs** for gateways and BGP events
- Align with **compliance frameworks** (ISO, NIST, CIS Benchmarks)

Monitoring and Troubleshooting

AZURE NETWORK WATCHER:

- IP flow verify
- VPN troubleshooting
- Packet capture
- Connection monitor

Azure Monitor Metrics:

- Tunnel up/down status
- Data throughput
- BGP peer status

KQL Query:

```
AzureDiagnostics

| where Category == "GatewayDiagnosticLog"

| where OperationName_s == "VpnTunnelConnected"
```

```
| summarize count() by bin(TimeGenerated, 1h)
```

Cost Considerations

Feature	VPN Gateway	ExpressRoute
Cost Model	Flat fee + data egress	Circuit fee + data transfer or unlimited
Performance	1–1.25 Gbps (VPNGw5)	Up to 10 Gbps
SLA	99.95%	99.95% (standard), 99.99% (premium)
Setup Time	Minutes to Hours	Days to Weeks (carrier dependent)

COST OPTIMIZATION TIPS:

- Use **MeteredData** for bursty workloads
- Schedule non-peak data transfers
- Apply **ExpressRoute FastPath** only for critical latency scenarios

Summary

INTEGRATING HYBRID networks with Azure using ExpressRoute and VPN Gateways enables seamless, secure communication between on-premises infrastructure and cloud resources. Understanding the strengths, trade-offs, and deployment patterns of these technologies empowers Azure architects to create resilient, performant, and scalable enterprise architectures.

Architectural Best Practices:

- Use **VPN Gateway** for quick, cost-effective hybrid connections

- Adopt **ExpressRoute** for mission-critical, high-volume traffic
- Combine both for reliability and migration flexibility
- Configure **BGP** for dynamic routing and resilience
- Use **Hub-and-Spoke** or **Virtual WAN** topologies for large environments
- Monitor continuously and test failover paths regularly

In the next chapter, we transition from infrastructure foundations to application-level architectures, exploring how to design microservices, serverless patterns, and modern event-driven systems using Azure-native tools and services.

Chapter 6: Designing Application Architectures

Building Microservices with Azure Kubernetes Service (AKS)

MICROSERVICES ARCHITECTURE is a modern approach to designing distributed applications that are modular, scalable, and resilient. In a microservices design, applications are composed of loosely coupled services that communicate over lightweight protocols and can be deployed, scaled, and updated independently. Microsoft Azure provides a robust platform for building and managing microservices through **Azure Kubernetes Service (AKS)**—a fully managed Kubernetes service that simplifies the deployment and operations of containerized applications.

This section provides a comprehensive guide to architecting, deploying, and managing microservices on AKS. It covers design principles, service mesh integration, CI/CD strategies, observability, scaling, security, and DevOps practices for a resilient, cloud-native application landscape.

Microservices Architecture Fundamentals

A MICROSERVICES ARCHITECTURE decomposes an application into discrete services, each responsible for a specific business capability. These services:

- Are independently deployable and versioned
- Have their own data store and bounded context
- Communicate over HTTP, gRPC, or messaging (e.g., AMQP)

- Are stateless or manage state externally
- Are polyglot and can be implemented in different languages or stacks

Advantages:

- Accelerated development and deployment
- Fine-grained scalability
- Fault isolation
- Easier CI/CD pipelines
- Flexibility in technology choices

Why Azure Kubernetes Service (AKS)?

AKS provides a managed Kubernetes environment, eliminating the operational overhead of cluster setup, scaling, and maintenance.

Key Features:

- Integrated with Azure AD for RBAC
- Node pool autoscaling
- Built-in monitoring with Azure Monitor
- Spot and Reserved nodes
- ARM, Bicep, and Terraform integration
- Support for GPUs, confidential compute, and Windows containers

Architectural Benefits:

- Run highly available, multi-tenant microservices
- Implement blue-green or canary deployments
- Integrate with service meshes like Istio or Open Service Mesh (OSM)
- Use persistent volumes with Azure Disks and Files

Microservices Architecture Pattern on AKS

TYPICAL ARCHITECTURE:

Ingress Controller

└─ Frontend Service

└─ API Gateway (optional)

├─ Auth Service

├─ User Service

├─ Orders Service

├─ Inventory Service

└─ Notification Service

Infrastructure Components:

- **Kubernetes Deployments** and **Services**
- **Horizontal Pod Autoscaler** for elasticity
- **Persistent Volumes** for stateful components
- **Azure Key Vault** integration for secrets

- **Prometheus + Grafana** or Azure Monitor for observability

Deploying AKS Cluster (CLI)

AZ AKS CREATE \

—resource-group rg-app \

—name myAKSCluster \

—node-count 3 \

—enable-addons monitoring \

—generate-ssh-keys \

—enable-managed-identity

Add Node Pool for Dev or GPU Workloads:

az aks nodepool add \

—resource-group rg-app \

—cluster-name myAKSCluster \

—name devpool \

—node-count 1 \

—node-vm-size Standard_DS2_v2 \

—mode User

Containerizing Microservices

EACH MICROSERVICE IS built and packaged as a container image.

Dockerfile Example:

```
FROM node:18

WORKDIR /app

COPY package*.json ./

RUN npm install

COPY . .

EXPOSE 3000

CMD ["node", "index.js"]
```

Push to Azure Container Registry (ACR):

```
az acr login—name myacr

docker tag user-service myacr.azurecr.io/user-service:v1

docker push myacr.azurecr.io/user-service:v1
```

Create Kubernetes Deployment YAML:

```
apiVersion: apps/v1

kind: Deployment

metadata:

name: user-service

spec:

replicas: 3

selector:
```

matchLabels:

app: user

template:

metadata:

labels:

app: user

spec:

containers:

- name: user

image: myacr.azurecr.io/user-service:v1

ports:

- containerPort: 3000

CI/CD Integration for AKS

USE **GitHub Actions**, **Azure DevOps Pipelines**, or **Flux** for GitOps to automate deployments.

Sample GitHub Workflow:

name: Deploy to AKS

on:

push:

branches: [main]

```
jobs:
build:
runs-on: ubuntu-latest
steps:
- uses: actions/checkout@v3
- uses: azure/docker-login@v1
with:
login-server: myacr.azurecr.io
username: ${{ secrets.ACR_USERNAME }}
password: ${{ secrets.ACR_PASSWORD }}
- run: |
docker build -t myacr.azurecr.io/user-service:${{ github.sha }} .
docker push myacr.azurecr.io/user-service:${{ github.sha }}
- uses: Azure/k8s-deploy@v1
with:
manifests: manifests/
images: |
myacr.azurecr.io/user-service:${{ github.sha }}
```

Service Mesh Integration

ADD A **service mesh** to manage microservice communication, security, and observability.

Open Service Mesh (OSM):

Add OSM extension:

az aks enable-addons—addons open-service-mesh—name myAKSCluster—resource-group rg-app

•

Benefits:

- mTLS between services
- Traffic shifting (canary, A/B)
- Telemetry collection
- Policy enforcement

Observability and Monitoring

USE **Azure Monitor**, **Prometheus**, and **Grafana** to monitor cluster and application health.

Enable Monitoring at Cluster Creation:

az aks create \

—enable-addons monitoring \

—workspace-resource-id <log-analytics-id>

Recommended Metrics:

- CPU/Memory per Pod
- Request latency
- Error rates (5xx, 4xx)
- Pod restart counts
- Queue lengths (if using messaging)

KQL Query Example:

```
KubePodInventory
| where ClusterName == "myAKSCluster" and ContainerStatus != "Running"
| summarize count() by ContainerName, ContainerStatus, bin(TimeGenerated, 1h)
```

Networking in AKS

KEY COMPONENTS:

- **Kubernetes Services**: ClusterIP, NodePort, LoadBalancer
- **Ingress Controller**: NGINX, AGIC (Azure App Gateway)
- **Private Clusters**: Restrict API server access to VNet
- **CNI Networking**: Azure CNI or Kubenet

Ingress YAML Example:

```
apiVersion: networking.k8s.io/v1
kind: Ingress
metadata:
```

```
name: user-ingress
annotations:
nginx.ingress.kubernetes.io/rewrite-target: /
spec:
rules:
- host: user.myapp.com
http:
paths:
- path: /
pathType: Prefix
backend:
service:
name: user-service
port:
number: 3000
```

Security Best Practices

- USE **Managed Identity** for Azure resource access
- Enforce **RBAC** using Azure AD groups
- Use **Pod Security Policies** or **Azure Policy for AKS**
- Store secrets in **Azure Key Vault**, mounted via CSI Driver

- Enable **network policies** to restrict pod-to-pod traffic
- Regularly scan images using **Defender for Containers**

Scaling Microservices

USE **Horizontal Pod Autoscaler (HPA)** and **Cluster Autoscaler**:

```
apiVersion: autoscaling/v2
kind: HorizontalPodAutoscaler
metadata:
name: orders-hpa
spec:
scaleTargetRef:
apiVersion: apps/v1
kind: Deployment
name: orders
minReplicas: 2
maxReplicas: 10
metrics:
- type: Resource
resource:
name: cpu
target:
```

type: Utilization

averageUtilization: 60

Common Pitfalls and Remedies

Challenge	Solution
High Pod Startup Time	Use readiness/liveness probes and pre-warmed containers
Resource Contention	Set resource limits/requests properly per container
Network Latency in Service Calls	Implement service mesh with retries and circuit breakers
Image Drift	Adopt GitOps or image tag immutability
Secret Management	Use CSI Secret Store with Azure Key Vault
Downtime During Upgrades	Use rolling deployments, readiness probes, and deployment strategies

Summary

BUILDING MICROSERVICES with Azure Kubernetes Service (AKS) enables architects to deliver scalable, modular, and resilient applications that align with modern DevOps and cloud-native principles. AKS abstracts the complexity of Kubernetes while integrating tightly with Azure's ecosystem, offering robust security, automation, and observability.

Architectural Best Practices:

- Design each service to be stateless and independently deployable
- Use ACR, Helm, and GitOps for secure and consistent deployments

- Scale effectively with HPA, Cluster Autoscaler, and node pools
- Secure clusters with RBAC, network policies, and managed identities
- Monitor and trace services using Prometheus, Azure Monitor, and Logs
- Use a service mesh for inter-service communication and control

In the next section, we'll explore how to design serverless architectures using Azure Functions—ideal for event-driven, reactive, and cost-efficient workloads.

Leveraging Serverless Architectures with Azure Functions

SERVERLESS COMPUTING redefines the traditional development and deployment process by abstracting infrastructure management, enabling developers to focus on code and business logic. Azure Functions, Microsoft's serverless compute platform, allows you to build event-driven applications that scale automatically and are billed only for actual execution time. This model is ideal for short-lived processes, reactive systems, real-time integrations, and micro-automation tasks that benefit from flexibility and cost-efficiency.

This section explores how to design, build, deploy, and manage serverless applications using Azure Functions. It includes best practices for architecture, binding types, scaling, state management, security, CI/CD, observability, and hybrid integration. You'll learn how to use Azure Functions as a foundation for modern, decoupled, cloud-native services.

What is Serverless Architecture?

SERVERLESS ARCHITECTURE refers to a design pattern where application components are hosted in a fully managed environment, eliminating the need to manage servers or runtime infrastructure.

Core Characteristics:

- **Event-driven**: Triggered by events such as HTTP requests, message queues, timers, or storage changes.
- **Stateless**: Functions typically do not retain state between invocations.
- **Elastic**: Scales automatically based on demand.
- **Metered billing**: Pay only for the execution time and resources used.

Azure Function Highlights:

- Built-in support for **triggers** and **bindings**
- Supports multiple languages (C#, JavaScript, Python, Java, PowerShell)
- Integrated with other Azure services like Blob Storage, Event Grid, Service Bus
- Runs on both **Consumption Plan** and **Premium/Isolated Plans**

Use Cases for Azure Functions

Use Case	Description
HTTP APIs	Stateless REST endpoints or microservices
Event Processing	Responding to blob uploads, database changes, or queue messages
Scheduled Tasks	Timed jobs (e.g., cleanups, synchronizations, ETL pipelines)
Real-Time File or Data Processing	Stream processing with Cosmos DB, Event Hubs, IoT Hub
Automation	Triggering workflows for DevOps, alerting, or notifications
Backend for Mobile or Web Applications	Lightweight backend logic supporting frontend apps

Hosting Plans for Azure Functions

Plan Type	Features	Ideal For
Consumption Plan	Autoscaling, per-execution billing	Intermittent, unpredictable load
Premium Plan	VNET integration, pre-warmed instances	Medium load, low latency
Dedicated Plan	Runs on App Service Plan infrastructure	Enterprise workloads, hybrid
Isolated Plan	Private VNET, enhanced performance	High-security, compliance-bound

BILLING MODEL:

In the **Consumption Plan**, you are billed per GB-s and per million executions, whereas **Premium** provides fixed cost with faster cold starts and more memory.

Function Triggers and Bindings

AZURE FUNCTIONS ARE powered by **triggers** and **bindings**:

- **Trigger**: Defines how the function is invoked (HTTP, queue, timer, etc.)
- **Input Binding**: Reads data from a service (e.g., Blob, Table, Cosmos DB)
- **Output Binding**: Writes data to a service (e.g., Send message to Queue, write to DB)

Example: HTTP Trigger with Cosmos DB Output Binding (JavaScript):

```
module.exports = async function (context, req) {

const item = {

id: req.body.id,

name: req.body.name,

timestamp: new Date()

};

context.bindings.outputDocument = item;

context.res = {

status: 200,

body: "Document written successfully"

};

};
```

function.json Configuration:

```
{
"bindings": [
{
"authLevel": "function",
"type": "httpTrigger",
"direction": "in",
"name": "req",
"methods": ["post"]
},
{
"type": "http",
"direction": "out",
"name": "res"
},
{
"type": "cosmosDB",
"direction": "out",
"name": "outputDocument",
"databaseName": "appdb",
```

```
"collectionName": "items",
"connectionStringSetting": "CosmosDBConnection"
}
]
}
```

Developing and Deploying Azure Functions

LOCAL DEVELOPMENT TOOLS:

- **Visual Studio Code** with Azure Functions extension
- **Azure Functions Core Tools CLI**
- Support for GitHub Actions and Azure DevOps CI/CD pipelines

Create a Function App (CLI):

```
az functionapp create \
—resource-group rg-app \
—consumption-plan-location westeurope \
—runtime node \
—functions-version 4 \
—name myfunctionapp \
—storage-account mystorageacct
```

Deploy via CLI:

func azure functionapp publish myfunctionapp

CI/CD Integration Example (GitHub Actions):

jobs:

build-and-deploy:

runs-on: ubuntu-latest

steps:

- uses: actions/checkout@v3

- uses: Azure/functions-action@v1

with:

app-name: myfunctionapp

package: '.'

publish-profile: ${{ secrets.AZURE_FUNCTIONAPP_PUBLISH_PROFILE }}

Scaling and Performance

AZURE FUNCTIONS AUTOMATICALLY scale based on incoming event rate.

Consumption Plan Scaling:

- Maximum of 200 instances per function app
- 1.5 GB memory limit per function execution
- Function timeout: 5 minutes (extendable to 10)

Premium Plan Scaling:

- Avoid cold starts with pre-warmed instances
- Longer execution duration (unlimited)
- More memory and CPU

Scaling Factors:

- Queue length
- HTTP request rate
- Timer intervals
- CPU/memory usage
- Custom metrics (Premium Plan with Azure Monitor)

Durable Functions for Stateful Workflows

DURABLE FUNCTIONS EXTEND Azure Functions by enabling stateful orchestration of workflows.

Orchestration Patterns:

- **Function chaining**: Execute functions in sequence
- **Fan-out/fan-in**: Parallelize function execution and aggregate results
- **Async HTTP APIs**: Handle long-running operations
- **Timers and checkpoints**: Persist execution between function calls

Example: Orchestration Function (C#):

[FunctionName("Orchestrator")]

```
public static async Task<List<string>> RunOrchestrator(

[OrchestrationTrigger] IDurableOrchestrationContext context)

{

var outputs = new List<string>();

outputs.Add(await context.CallActivityAsync<string>("SayHello", "Tokyo"));

outputs.Add(await context.CallActivityAsync<string>("SayHello", "London"));

outputs.Add(await context.CallActivityAsync<string>("SayHello", "Seattle"));

return outputs;

}
```

Security Best Practices

- **Use Managed Identity** for accessing Azure services securely
- **Restrict access** with function-level or app-level authentication
- **Store secrets** in **Azure Key Vault**
- **Enable VNET integration** for backend services (Premium Plan)
- **Enforce HTTPS** on all endpoints
- **Enable Application Gateway or Azure API Management** in front of Functions

Observability and Diagnostics

AZURE FUNCTIONS INTEGRATE with **Application Insights** for monitoring.

Key Metrics:

- Execution count
- Execution duration
- Failures
- Cold start time
- Dependency tracking

KQL Example: Failed Function Invocations:

```
requests
| where success == false
| summarize count() by name, bin(timestamp, 5m)
```

Alerts and Dashboards:

- Configure alerts on error rate or high latency
- Visualize throughput and failures in custom dashboards

Cost Optimization

CONSUMPTION PLAN:

- Ideal for intermittent workloads
- Billed per execution and GB-s

- First 1 million executions/month free

Premium Plan:

- Suited for predictable or enterprise workloads
- Avoids cold starts and supports VNET integration

Tips:

- Use durable timers for long-wait scenarios
- Set retry policies instead of repeated polling
- Optimize bindings to avoid unnecessary reads/writes

Integration with Other Azure Services

Service	Integration Pattern
Azure Event Grid	Event-driven triggers
Azure Logic Apps	Chaining Functions within workflows
Azure API Management	Abstract and secure function endpoints
Azure Key Vault	Secure secrets and keys
Azure Cosmos DB	Trigger on inserts or update documents
Azure Storage	React to blob uploads or queue messages

Summary

AZURE FUNCTIONS ENABLE architects to design highly responsive, cost-efficient, and scalable applications without worrying about server provisioning and maintenance. Whether building APIs, automation workflows, or data processing pipelines, Functions offer unmatched speed and agility for modern cloud-native development.

Architectural Guidelines:

- Use serverless for short-lived, event-driven processes
- Choose the right hosting plan based on latency and throughput needs
- Use triggers and bindings to simplify integration with other services
- Adopt Durable Functions for complex workflows
- Monitor performance and failures using Application Insights
- Secure your apps using identity, encryption, and network isolation

In the next section, we will explore how to integrate and manage APIs using Azure API Management and Logic Apps, enabling secure, scalable, and observable interfaces between internal systems and external consumers.

API Management and Integration with Logic Apps

MODERN APPLICATIONS are increasingly built as modular, loosely coupled components that interact through APIs and automation. These integrations may span internal services, partner ecosystems, legacy systems, SaaS platforms, and cloud-native applications. To ensure secure, scalable, and maintainable connectivity, Azure provides two powerful services: **Azure API Management (APIM)** and **Azure Logic Apps**. Together, they form a comprehensive integration platform capable of handling diverse workloads with consistency, policy enforcement, and workflow automation.

This section details how to architect, deploy, and govern APIs using APIM, and how to orchestrate data and system interactions using

Logic Apps. You will learn about service virtualization, API versioning, throttling, custom policies, enterprise connectors, and hybrid integration patterns essential for scalable application architectures.

Role of APIs and Integration in Cloud Architectures

APIS PROVIDE A STANDARDIZED way for services to communicate. They are central to:

- Service-oriented and microservices architectures
- B2B integrations and partner connectivity
- Mobile and web app backends
- Third-party data exchange
- Internal app modernization efforts

Integration platforms like **Logic Apps** help automate and coordinate tasks across APIs and systems, forming **low-code/no-code business processes** and **event-driven workflows**.

Azure API Management (APIM): Overview

AZURE API MANAGEMENT provides a centralized platform to expose, manage, secure, and analyze APIs. It acts as a **gateway** and **proxy layer** between consumers and backend services.

Core Components:

- **API Gateway** – handles traffic routing, throttling, caching, and transformation
- **Developer Portal** – self-service portal for developers to discover and consume APIs

- **Publisher Portal** – admin interface for managing APIs, revisions, and versions
- **Policy Engine** – allows fine-grained control over requests and responses

Supported API Backends:

- Azure Functions, App Services, AKS
- On-premises APIs via VPN/ExpressRoute
- SaaS services (Salesforce, Dynamics)
- Any REST, SOAP, or GraphQL endpoint

APIM Tiers and Use Cases

Tier	Features	Use Cases
Developer	Low-cost, non-production use	Testing and dev teams
Basic	Production use with lower SLA	Small to medium applications
Standard	Medium-scale APIs, VNET support	Enterprise APIs with regional access
Premium	Multi-region deployment, VNET, hybrid connectivity	Global apps, hybrid integration, B2B, regulated industries

Deploying API Management (CLI Example)

AZ APIM CREATE \

—name my-apim \

—resource-group rg-integration \

—publisher-email admin@mydomain.com \

—publisher-name "My Company" \

—sku-name Consumption \

—location uksouth

Importing and Publishing APIs

APIS CAN BE IMPORTED into APIM via:

- OpenAPI (Swagger) specs
- WSDL files (for SOAP APIs)
- Azure Functions / App Services
- Git repos (APIM DevOps Toolkit)

az apim api import \

—resource-group rg-integration \

—service-name my-apim \

—path users \

—api-id user-api \

—specification-format OpenApi \

—specification-path ./openapi.json

Policies and Security

POLICIES CONTROL API behavior without changing backend code.

Examples:

- **Rate limiting** – prevent abuse
- **IP filtering** – block or allow traffic
- **Rewrite URL/query** – transform parameters
- **Header injection** – add authentication tokens
- **JWT validation** – enforce token-based access

Policy Example (XML):

```
<inbound>

<rate-limit calls="100" renewal-period="60" />

<validate-jwt header-name="Authorization" failed-validation-httpcode="401" require-scheme="Bearer">

<openid-config url="https://login.microsoftonline.com/common/v2.0/.well-known/openid-configuration" />

<audiences>

<audience>api://my-api</audience>

</audiences>

</validate-jwt>

</inbound>
```

API Versioning and Revisions

APIM SUPPORTS **versioning** and **revisions**:

- **Versions**: Major changes (URL, schema) – /v1/users, /v2/users

- **Revisions**: Minor updates (headers, query strings) – transparent to users

Versioning Methods:

- Path (/v1/)
- Header (api-version)
- Query parameter (?version=1.0)

Developer Portal

OUT-OF-THE-BOX CUSTOMIZABLE portal for API consumers:

- Auto-generated documentation (Swagger, test console)
- API key management
- Subscription management
- Custom branding and theming

Customization Options:

- Use the Developer Portal CMS
- Inject JavaScript/CSS for branding
- Connect to Azure AD B2C or external identity providers

Logic Apps: Overview and Use Cases

AZURE LOGIC APPS is a serverless workflow engine that connects disparate services using visual design or code-first approaches.

Use Cases:

- Orchestrating multi-step business processes
- Event-driven automation (e.g., file ingestion, email triggers)
- Connecting legacy on-prem systems with cloud services
- ETL and data synchronization tasks
- Approval workflows and human-in-the-loop automation

Logic App Components

- **Triggers**: Start the workflow (e.g., HTTP, timer, file creation)
- **Actions**: Tasks or steps (e.g., call REST API, send email, insert DB record)
- **Connectors**: Integrations with 600+ services including Office 365, Salesforce, SAP, ServiceNow
- **Control Flow**: Conditionals, loops, switch cases, scopes, error handling

---

Building a Logic App (Visual Designer or Code)

EXAMPLE: HTTP TRIGGER → Blob Upload → Email Alert

1. HTTP request received
2. Parse JSON payload
3. Upload data to Blob Storage
4. Send email via Outlook

ARM Template Snippet:

```
{
```

```
"type": "Microsoft.Logic/workflows",
"apiVersion": "2019-05-01",
"name": "uploadProcessor",
"location": "uksouth",
"properties": {
"definition": {
"$schema": "https://schema.management.azure.com/providers/Microsoft.Logic/schemas/2016-06-01/workflowdefinition.json#",
"triggers": {
"http": {
"type": "Request",
"kind": "Http",
"inputs": {
"schema": { "type": "object", "properties": { "file": { "type": "string" } } }
}
}
},
"actions": {
"upload": {
"type": "ApiConnection",
"inputs": {
```

```
"host": { "connectionName": "azureblob", "operationId": "UploadFile" },

"parameters": { "path": "uploads/file.txt", "content": "@triggerBody()?['file']" }

}

},

"email": {

"type": "ApiConnection",

"inputs": {

"host": { "connectionName": "office365", "operationId": "SendEmail" },

"parameters": {

"to": "admin@mydomain.com",

"subject": "File Received",

"body": "A file was uploaded to blob storage."

}

}

}

}

}

}
```

}

Enterprise Integration with Logic Apps

- **On-prem Data Gateway**: Connect securely to SQL Server, SAP, Oracle, etc.
- **B2B and EDI Integration**: Supports X12, EDIFACT, AS2 for trading partners
- **Hybrid Connectors**: Combine cloud and on-prem data using Hybrid Worker
- **Integration Accounts**: Manage maps, schemas, partners, and certificates

Monitoring and Governance

APIM MONITORING:

- Integrates with Azure Monitor and Log Analytics
- Metrics: call count, latency, response codes
- Diagnostics: request tracing and event hub export
- Auditing: subscription, key usage, throttling

Logic Apps Monitoring:

- Run history and real-time status
- Trigger failures and retries
- Integration with Azure Application Insights
- Custom alerts and dashboards

KQL Sample for APIM Logs:

```
AzureDiagnostics

| where ResourceType == "APIMGatewayLogs"

| summarize count() by apiId_s, httpStatus_d, bin(TimeGenerated, 1h)
```

Security Considerations

- USE **APIM policies** to validate tokens and restrict IPs
- Use **VNET Integration** for Logic Apps Standard
- Store credentials in **Azure Key Vault**
- Authenticate Logic Apps using **Managed Identity**
- Encrypt sensitive outputs and trigger data

DevOps and CI/CD Integration

- USE **ARM/Bicep**, **Terraform**, or **Azure DevOps Pipelines**
- APIM **Git integration** for API definitions and policies
- Logic Apps (Standard) supports **Visual Studio Code**, GitHub workflows
- Automate deployments with environments and release pipelines

---

Summary

API MANAGEMENT AND Logic Apps are foundational tools for any Azure integration strategy. While APIM ensures controlled, discoverable, and secure access to APIs, Logic Apps orchestrate business processes across heterogeneous systems with minimal code. Combined, they enable scalable, modular, and intelligent application architectures.

Architectural Guidelines:

- Use **APIM** to abstract, secure, and version backend APIs
- Expose APIs to partners and internal developers via Developer Portal
- Apply **policies** for throttling, transformation, and security
- Use **Logic Apps** for visual workflow integration and automation
- Combine Logic Apps with APIs to build powerful composite services
- Monitor and govern with Azure Monitor, Log Analytics, and alerts
- Secure with **identity**, **encryption**, and **network isolation**

In the next section, we will delve into building event-driven systems with Azure Event Grid and Service Bus to enable scalable, decoupled, and reactive cloud-native architectures.

Event-Driven Design Patterns with Event Grid and Service Bus

MODERN APPLICATIONS must be responsive, loosely coupled, and scalable to meet evolving user demands and integration needs. Traditional tightly-coupled architectures often lead to inflexible systems with scaling and maintenance challenges. **Event-driven architectures (EDA)** solve this by promoting asynchronous, decoupled communication through events. In Azure, two core services enable robust EDA implementations: **Azure Event Grid** and **Azure Service Bus**.

This section focuses on designing, implementing, and managing event-driven systems using Azure's messaging services. You'll learn when to use Event Grid or Service Bus, how to apply architectural patterns like pub/sub, queue-based load leveling, fan-out/fan-in, and event sourcing, as well as security, delivery guarantees, and monitoring best practices.

Introduction to Event-Driven Architecture (EDA)

EVENT-DRIVEN ARCHITECTURE is a design model in which components communicate by producing and consuming events. Events are records of something that has happened in the system, and event producers and consumers operate independently, connected through event brokers.

Key Benefits:

- Decoupling between producers and consumers
- Scalability through asynchronous message flow
- Resiliency through retries and dead-lettering
- Extensibility by adding consumers without modifying producers

Core Concepts:

- **Event**: Notification about a state change
- **Publisher**: Component that emits events
- **Subscriber**: Component that listens and responds to events

- **Event Broker**: Middleware that routes events (e.g., Event Grid, Service Bus)

Azure Event Grid

AZURE EVENT GRID is a fully managed, real-time event routing service built for high throughput and low latency.

Use Cases:

- Reacting to blob uploads or database updates
- Serverless automation (e.g., trigger Azure Functions)
- Real-time notifications
- Integrating with SaaS (e.g., Event Grid Partner Topics)

Supported Event Sources:

- Azure Blob Storage, Resource Groups, Event Hubs
- Custom applications via HTTP API
- Third-party services (e.g., GitHub, SAP)

Event Handlers:

- Azure Functions
- Logic Apps
- Event Hubs
- WebHooks
- Azure Automation

Event Types:

- **System Events**: Emitted by Azure services
- **Custom Events**: Defined by applications
- **Partner Events**: Emitted by third-party services

Azure Service Bus

AZURE SERVICE BUS is a reliable enterprise messaging service designed for complex integration patterns.

Use Cases:

- Decoupling microservices with reliable queues
- Ordered, durable messaging with exactly-once delivery
- Command and control messaging
- Request-response patterns

Key Features:

- **Queues**: Point-to-point communication
- **Topics and Subscriptions**: Publish-subscribe model
- **Sessions**: Maintain message order
- **Dead-lettering**: Handle message delivery failures
- **Advanced filtering**: SQL-like rule-based routing

Comparison Table:

Feature	Event Grid	Service Bus
Pattern	Pub/Sub	Pub/Sub and Queue
Delivery	At least once	At most once / Exactly once (with dedupe)
Message size limit	1 MB	256 KB (Standard), 1 MB (Premium)
Ordering	Not guaranteed	Guaranteed with sessions
Latency	<100 ms	Higher (due to retries, sessions)
Use Case	Reactive events	Reliable commands/tasks

Architectural Patterns

1. Pub/Sub Pattern

IN THIS MODEL, AN EVENT is published and consumed by multiple services independently.

Use Event Grid for lightweight, fan-out pub/sub:

- Blob Storage uploads trigger thumbnail generation, audit logging, and email notifications
- One producer, multiple independent consumers

Use Service Bus Topics for durable delivery with filters:

- A new order event is sent to accounting, fulfillment, and customer service, each with its own filtered subscription

2. Queue-Based Load Leveling

A QUEUE ABSORBS BURSTS of requests and allows processing to continue asynchronously, helping maintain system stability.

Use Service Bus Queues to:

- Buffer API requests for background processing
- Decouple frontend requests from backend processors
- Scale processors based on queue depth

3. Fan-Out/Fan-In

DISTRIBUTE PROCESSING across multiple workers and aggregate results:

- Fan-out: Use Event Grid to trigger parallel Azure Functions
- Fan-in: Aggregate function results using Durable Functions or Azure Storage

4. Event Sourcing

CAPTURE CHANGES AS a series of immutable events instead of overwriting state.

- Store events in Event Hubs or Service Bus
- Replay events to rebuild state
- Use with CQRS for read/write separation

Event Grid Implementation Example

CREATE EVENT GRID TOPIC (CLI):

az eventgrid topic create \

—name app-events \

—resource-group rg-app \

—location uksouth

Publish Custom Event:

az eventgrid event publish \

—topic-name app-events \

—resource-group rg-app \

—event-id $(uuidgen) \

—event-type "UserCreated" \

—subject "/user/1234" \

—data '{ "id": 1234, "email": "user@example.com" }' \

—data-version 1.0

Subscribe with Azure Function:

az eventgrid event-subscription create \

—name userCreatedHandler \

—source-resource-id /subscriptions/.../topics/app-events \

—endpoint-type azurefunction \

—endpoint /subscriptions/.../functions/userHandler

Service Bus Implementation Example

CREATE QUEUE (CLI):

az servicebus namespace create \

—resource-group rg-app \

—name sb-app-namespace \

—location uksouth \

—sku Standard

az servicebus queue create \

—resource-group rg-app \

—namespace-name sb-app-namespace \

—name user-registration-queue

Send Message:

var sender = client.CreateSender("user-registration-queue");

await sender.SendMessageAsync(new ServiceBusMessage("{ \"id\": 1234, \"email\": \"user@example.com\" }"));

Receive Message (with session):

var sessionReceiver = await client.AcceptNextSessionAsync("user-registration-queue");

ServiceBusReceivedMessage message = await sessionReceiver.ReceiveMessageAsync();

Security and Governance

- USE **Managed Identity** for authentication
- Enforce **IP restrictions** on Event Grid subscriptions
- Store credentials securely in **Azure Key Vault**
- Apply **role-based access control (RBAC)** to namespaces and topics
- Encrypt messages in transit and at rest (Service Bus uses Azure Storage encryption)

Monitoring and Diagnostics

EVENT GRID MONITORING:

- Diagnostic settings for delivery failures
- Dead-lettering for undeliverable messages
- Azure Monitor integration

Service Bus Monitoring:

- Queue length, active and dead-letter message counts
- Failed delivery counts
- Integration with Log Analytics and Application Insights

KQL Example: Count Failed Deliveries (Service Bus):

```
AzureDiagnostics
| where Category == "ServiceBusLogs"
| where StatusCode_d == 500
```

```
| summarize count() by bin(TimeGenerated, 1h)
```

Event Reliability and Delivery Guarantees

Characteristic	Event Grid	Service Bus
Retry Policy	Exponential backoff	Configurable retries
Dead-lettering	Yes (subscription level)	Yes (queue/topic level)
Duplicate Detection	No	Yes (with message ID + TTL)
Message TTL	24h default	Configurable (up to 14 days)

DESIGN TIPS:

- Implement idempotent consumers
- Use correlation IDs for tracking
- Enable message logging for replay/debug

CI/CD and Infrastructure as Code

DEPLOY WITH ARM, BICEP, or Terraform:

- Event Grid Topics, Domains, Subscriptions
- Service Bus Namespaces, Queues, Topics, Authorization Rules

Bicep Example for Event Grid Topic:

```
resource topic 'Microsoft.EventGrid/topics@2021-12-01' = {

name: 'app-events'

location: resourceGroup().location
```

sku: {

name: 'Basic'

}

}

Best Practices:

- Use parameterized templates
- Store secrets in Key Vault and reference them securely
- Integrate deployment with Azure DevOps pipelines or GitHub Actions

---

Summary

EVENT-DRIVEN DESIGN is a cornerstone of scalable, loosely coupled, and resilient cloud applications. Azure Event Grid and Service Bus provide powerful mechanisms to implement asynchronous communication, reactive automation, and complex orchestration between microservices, systems, and users.

Architectural Guidelines:

- Use **Event Grid** for lightweight, high-throughput, fan-out scenarios
- Use **Service Bus** when you need ordering, deduplication, or transactional guarantees
- Apply **pub/sub**, **queueing**, and **event sourcing** patterns appropriately

- Monitor and troubleshoot using **Log Analytics**, **Azure Monitor**, and **Application Insights**
- Secure endpoints with **RBAC**, **Managed Identities**, and **Key Vault**
- Build infrastructure using **ARM**, **Bicep**, or **Terraform**, integrated into CI/CD

In the next section, we'll focus on observability and performance tuning using Application Insights and best practices to instrument distributed applications in Azure.

Application Insights and Performance Monitoring

IN MODERN CLOUD-NATIVE architectures, observability is not optional—it is essential. To ensure optimal application health, diagnose performance bottlenecks, monitor usage trends, and trace user interactions, developers and architects need a robust monitoring solution. **Azure Application Insights** is a powerful application performance management (APM) service that provides deep diagnostics and telemetry across distributed applications.

This section provides comprehensive guidance on integrating Application Insights into Azure-hosted applications, interpreting performance telemetry, creating custom dashboards and alerts, enabling distributed tracing across services, and leveraging telemetry for tuning and optimization. It also covers integration with Azure Monitor, Log Analytics, and development workflows to establish a complete observability strategy.

The Role of Monitoring in Cloud Applications

MONITORING ADDRESSES several key concerns in production environments:

- **Reliability**: Is the app up and serving users reliably?
- **Performance**: Are latency and response times acceptable?
- **User Experience**: What paths are users taking? Where are they dropping off?
- **Capacity Planning**: Are resources scaling appropriately?
- **Security and Compliance**: Are there anomalous patterns or unauthorized accesses?

Observability encompasses three pillars:

1. **Metrics**: Time-series measurements of system state (CPU, memory, requests)
2. **Logs**: Structured/semi-structured event data (errors, audit logs)
3. **Traces**: End-to-end records of request flows across services

Application Insights is designed to collect and correlate all three.

Overview of Azure Application Insights

APPLICATION INSIGHTS can be used with:

- Azure App Service
- Azure Functions
- Azure Kubernetes Service (AKS)

- Virtual Machines and containers
- JavaScript frontends (React, Angular, Vue)
- APIs and backend services (.NET, Java, Node.js, Python, etc.)

Core Features:

- Automatic request and exception tracking
- Dependency monitoring (HTTP, SQL, Redis, etc.)
- Live metrics stream
- Application map visualization
- Availability tests (URL pings, multi-step web tests)
- Integration with Azure DevOps, GitHub, and ITSM tools

Instrumenting Applications

Automatic Instrumentation

AZURE APP SERVICE AND Functions provide **auto-instrumentation** for .NET, Java, and Node.js apps.

- Simply enable **Application Insights** in the Azure portal
- No code changes required
- Auto-collects requests, exceptions, dependencies, and traces

```
az webapp update \
—name myapp \
—resource-group rg-app \
```

—set siteConfig.alwaysOn=true \

—set appSettings="[{'name':'APPINSIGHTS_INSTRUMENTATIONKEY','va

Manual SDK Integration

FOR ADVANCED SCENARIOS, install the Application Insights SDK.

.NET Example:

```
Install-Package Microsoft.ApplicationInsights.AspNetCore

public void ConfigureServices(IServiceCollection services)

{

services.AddApplicationInsightsTelemetry();

}
```

Node.js Example:

```
npm install applicationinsights

const appInsights = require("applicationinsights");

appInsights.setup("<instrumentation_key>").start();
```

Frontend (JavaScript):

```
<script type="text/javascript">

var appInsights=window.appInsights||function(config){

function r(config){t[config]=function(){var i=arguments;t.queue.push(function(){t[config].apply(t,i)})}}
```

```
var
t={config:config},u=document,e=window,o="script",s=u.createElement(

for(s.src=config.url||"https://az416426.vo.msecnd.net/scripts/b/
ai.2.min.js",u.getElementsByTagName(o)[0].parentNode.appendChild(s),

return t;

}({

instrumentationKey:"<INSTRUMENTATION_KEY>"

});

window.appInsights=appInsights;

</script>
```

Analyzing Performance Metrics

KEY OUT-OF-THE-BOX metrics include:

Metric	Description
Server Response Time	Time to process requests
Failed Requests	Number and % of unsuccessful HTTP calls
Dependency Duration	Time spent in external dependencies (SQL, REST)
Exceptions	Unhandled errors across services
Availability	% of successful synthetic tests

Custom Events:

```
TelemetryClient telemetry = new TelemetryClient();

telemetry.TrackEvent("CheckoutStarted", new Dictionary<string,
string> { { "CartSize", "4" } });
```

Distributed Tracing

WHEN BUILDING MICROSERVICES or distributed APIs, tracing requests across services is vital for debugging and optimization.

Enable Distributed Tracing:

- Use **Correlation IDs** in HTTP headers
- Use Request-Id and Correlation-Context headers
- In AKS, install **Azure Monitor for Containers** to auto-inject tracing
- In Azure Functions and App Service, enable Application Insights integration

End-to-End View Includes:

- Caller and callee services
- External dependencies (SQL, REST APIs)
- Latency breakdown by component
- Failure points and exception traces

Application Map

APPLICATION MAP shows a real-time visual of service dependencies:

- Nodes represent services or components
- Arrows show latency and throughput
- Red lines indicate errors or degraded performance

Use this for:

- Understanding service topology
- Identifying hot paths and bottlenecks
- Detecting service outages or misrouting

Workbooks and Dashboards

WORKBOOKS PROVIDE CUSTOMIZABLE dashboards for telemetry data.

Use Cases:

- SLA dashboards
- Business KPIs (conversion rates, cart abandonment)
- Performance heatmaps
- Security incident tracking

Create via Portal:

- Go to Application Insights → Workbooks → New
- Add visualizations: charts, tables, gauges
- Use KQL queries to filter and aggregate

Writing Kusto Queries (KQL)

BASIC EXAMPLE – SLOWEST Endpoints:

```
requests

| where success == true
```

```
| summarize avg(duration) by name
| top 10 by avg_duration desc
```

Failed Dependencies:

```
dependencies
| where success == false
| summarize count() by target, type, resultCode
```

Correlating Errors with User Sessions:

```
exceptions
| join kind=inner (
requests
| project operation_Id, url
) on operation_Id
| summarize count() by url, type
```

Availability and Synthetic Testing

CREATE URL PING TESTS to verify:

- Endpoint health
- DNS resolution
- SSL certificate validity
- Geographic availability

Alert on failures or performance degradation using action groups.

CLI Example:

```
az monitor app-insights web-test create \
—resource-group rg-app \
—name HomepageTest \
—location "uksouth" \
—enabled true \
—frequency 300 \
—timeout 30 \
—web-test-kind ping \
—web-test-name "homepage-test" \
—url "https://myapp.azurewebsites.net"
```

Alerting and Anomaly Detection

APPLICATION INSIGHTS integrates with **Azure Monitor Alerts**:

- Set alerts for CPU, failures, load time, or user sessions
- Use **Smart Detection** for anomalies and trends
- Trigger workflows via **Logic Apps**, **Azure Automation**, or **email/SMS**

Example Alert Rule:

- Condition: Server response time > 1 sec for 5 minutes
- Action: Email DevOps team + trigger redeployment workflow

DevOps Integration

- ANNOTATE TELEMETRY with **deployment markers** from Azure DevOps
- Automate alert-based scaling or failover
- Export telemetry to **Log Analytics** for long-term storage
- Integrate with **Grafana**, **Power BI**, or **Elastic**

Cost Optimization and Retention

- DEFAULT DATA RETENTION is 90 days (configurable)
- Reduce ingestion by sampling or filtering unneeded telemetry
- Use **Adaptive Sampling** to automatically reduce data volume
- Export critical logs only via Diagnostic Settings

Example: Enable Adaptive Sampling in .NET:

```
services.ConfigureTelemetryModule<AdaptiveSamplingTelemetryProcessor
o) =>

{

module.MaxTelemetryItemsPerSecond = 5;

});
```

Summary

AZURE APPLICATION INSIGHTS is a foundational tool for monitoring, diagnosing, and optimizing application performance in the cloud. By integrating it into every layer of your architecture—from frontend to backend, across microservices and serverless functions—you gain full visibility into application behavior and health.

Architectural Guidelines:

- Enable **Application Insights** across all services (App Service, AKS, Functions)
- Use **automatic instrumentation** wherever possible
- Track **custom events** and metrics for business KPIs
- Implement **distributed tracing** to follow user journeys
- Use **Workbooks**, **KQL**, and **Application Maps** to visualize insights
- Set proactive **alerts** and use **Smart Detection**
- Optimize data retention and ingestion to control cost

In the next chapter, we'll shift our focus to preparing for the AZ-305 exam—reviewing objectives, walkthroughs, and strategies to help you succeed with confidence.

Chapter 7: Preparing for the AZ-305 Exam

Understanding the Exam Format and Objectives

THE AZ-305 EXAM, OFFICIALLY titled **"Designing Microsoft Azure Infrastructure Solutions,"** is a critical milestone for professionals aiming to become Microsoft Certified: Azure Solutions Architects. The exam tests candidates on their ability to design cloud and hybrid solutions that run on Microsoft Azure, including aspects related to compute, network, storage, monitoring, identity, and security. It validates not only your theoretical understanding but your practical architectural capabilities.

In this section, we'll explore the structure of the AZ-305 exam, its detailed objective domains, scoring mechanics, question types, exam prerequisites, and key preparation strategies to ensure you're fully equipped to pass with confidence.

Overview of the Certification Path

THE AZ-305 EXAM IS part of the requirements for the **Microsoft Certified: Azure Solutions Architect Expert** certification. To achieve this credential, candidates must:

1. **Pass Exam AZ-305**: Focused on designing Azure infrastructure.
2. **Hold a current associate-level certification** (typically AZ-104: Microsoft Azure Administrator Associate).

Target Audience:

- Cloud Architects
- Infrastructure Engineers
- DevOps Engineers with architecture responsibilities
- Consultants and technical leads managing Azure projects

Skills Validated:

- Designing identity, governance, and monitoring solutions
- Designing data storage solutions
- Designing business continuity strategies
- Designing infrastructure solutions
- Designing application architectures and integrations

Exam Format and Delivery

Attribute	Details
Exam Code	AZ-305
Duration	100–120 minutes
Question Count	40–60 (varies by delivery)
Passing Score	700 / 1000
Cost	USD $165 (subject to regional pricing)
Delivery	Pearson VUE (online proctored or test center)
Language Availability	English, Japanese, Chinese, German, French, and others

SCORING:

- No negative marking
- Each question contributes equally unless stated otherwise

- Case studies may carry grouped weighting

Exam Structure:

1. **Single-choice and multiple-choice questions**
2. **Case studies** with sets of scenario-based questions
3. **Drag-and-drop** solutions into correct steps or designs
4. **Hot area** questions to select correct configuration options
5. **Best answer** selection from a set of plausible solutions

---

Exam Objective Domains

AS OF THE LATEST MICROSOFT exam skills outline, AZ-305 covers four major functional areas:

1. Design Identity, Governance, and Monitoring Solutions (25–30%)

- AZURE AD TENANT and identity strategy
- Role-based access control (RBAC)
- Azure Policy and resource governance
- Monitoring and alerting via Azure Monitor and Log Analytics
- Security baselines and compliance enforcement

2. Design Data Storage Solutions (20–25%)

- SELECTING STORAGE account types
- Designing access control and redundancy strategies
- Data lake and blob storage usage

- Integration with database services (Azure SQL, Cosmos DB, etc.)
- Archival and lifecycle policies

3. Design Business Continuity Solutions (10–15%)

- RPO AND RTO REQUIREMENT planning
- High availability and resiliency patterns
- Disaster recovery using Azure Backup and Site Recovery
- Geo-redundant and zone-redundant architectures
- Application-level resiliency

4. Design Infrastructure Solutions (30–35%)

- VIRTUAL NETWORKING and subnet strategies
- Hybrid connectivity using VPN, ExpressRoute, VNet peering
- Compute workload deployment (VMs, containers, App Services)
- Network security, routing, and firewall configuration
- Application scaling and elasticity

Each domain is weighted, so it's crucial to focus study time in proportion to these percentages.

Understanding the Case Study Format

AZ-305 FREQUENTLY INCLUDES case studies that simulate real-world design challenges.

Structure:

- Introductory scenario with business and technical requirements
- Diagrams of current and target-state architecture
- Follow-up questions testing ability to:
    - Select appropriate Azure services
    - Prioritize design trade-offs
    - Align design to compliance and budget constraints

Tips:

- Don't overthink—answers must align with scenario goals
- Some questions restrict the back/forward navigation
- Read all requirements before answering

Depth vs Breadth of Knowledge

THE EXAM DOES NOT EXPECT deep specialization in any one Azure service but rather the ability to **synthesize multiple services into a cohesive solution.** This includes:

- Knowing when to use Azure SQL vs Cosmos DB
- Choosing between App Service, AKS, or Functions
- Designing hybrid models with ExpressRoute and VPN Gateway
- Understanding high availability (HA) options at each tier
- Applying monitoring and governance at enterprise scale

Design Mindset Required:

- Prioritize **business requirements** (SLA, scalability, cost)
- Evaluate **trade-offs** (PaaS vs IaaS, performance vs complexity)
- Design for **security and compliance**
- Understand **multi-region deployment** strategies

How AZ-305 Differs from AZ-104 or AZ-700

Exam	Role Tested	Focus
AZ-104	Azure Administrator	Operational knowledge: deploy, configure
AZ-700	Azure Network Engineer	Deep network architecture and routing
AZ-305	Azure Solutions Architect (Design Role)	Holistic system design and trade-offs

YOU'RE EXPECTED TO know **what to design** rather than how to execute CLI commands or build pipelines step-by-step.

Preparation Strategies

1. MICROSOFT LEARN Path:

Follow the official AZ-305 Learning Path:

- https://learn.microsoft.com/en-us/certifications/exams/az-305/

2. Practice Labs and Sandboxes:

- Set up a free Azure account or use Azure for Students
- Deploy VNets, Functions, Cosmos DB, AKS clusters
- Configure monitoring, diagnostics, and role assignments

3. Whiteboard Design Sessions:

- Practice sketching solutions to prompts like:
  - "Design a solution for global e-commerce site with data sovereignty"
  - "Design a hybrid cloud for a banking application"

4. Focus on Core Patterns:

- Multi-region failover
- Event-driven and microservice architecture
- Identity federation and conditional access
- Monitoring and logging via Azure Monitor and Log Analytics
- Data partitioning and lifecycle management

5. Practice Exams:

- Use MeasureUp or Whizlabs for timed simulation tests
- Review explanations—especially incorrect ones—to identify weak spots

---

What to Expect on Exam Day

- SHOW UP EARLY OR check your online exam environment
- Bring a valid ID (passport, driver's license)
- For online proctoring, ensure webcam, lighting, and desk compliance
- Expect no breaks during the exam

- Use **flags** to mark questions to revisit (when allowed)
- Use scratchpad/whiteboard provided for visualizing architecture

Post-Exam Recommendations

- REVIEW THE PERFORMANCE report immediately
- Identify weaker domains for follow-up study
- Consider writing blog posts or giving talks to reinforce your learning
- Pursue **AZ-400 (DevOps Engineer Expert)** or specialty certs like **AZ-720 (Support Engineer)** or **SC-100 (Cybersecurity Architect)** if aligned with your career

Summary

THE AZ-305 EXAM IS more than a test—it's a validation of your ability to design robust, scalable, and secure Azure solutions across a variety of business scenarios. It challenges you to balance cost, performance, availability, and governance, making architectural decisions based on real-world trade-offs. Understanding the exam structure, mastering the objective domains, and practicing hands-on design are the keys to passing.

Key Takeaways:

- AZ-305 is case-study and scenario-driven
- Design knowledge is tested across identity, storage, networking, continuity, and monitoring
- Hands-on labs and whiteboarding exercises are essential

- Expect broad questions requiring judgment, not rote memorization
- Think like a **solution architect**, not just a cloud engineer

In the next section, we will dive into practical practice question walkthroughs that mirror the AZ-305 exam style—providing not just answers, but the reasoning and architectural thinking behind each choice.

Practice Question Walkthroughs

ONE OF THE MOST EFFECTIVE ways to prepare for the AZ-305 exam is by working through detailed practice questions that mirror the style, structure, and complexity of the real exam. Unlike typical certification quizzes, AZ-305 challenges your architectural decision-making across ambiguous and multifaceted scenarios. This section provides a set of advanced practice questions followed by in-depth walkthroughs of each answer, highlighting critical thinking, trade-offs, and alignment with Microsoft's design principles.

These walkthroughs are not only a tool for checking your answers, but a way to internalize the **design mindset** needed to succeed in the exam and in real-world cloud architecture.

Practice Scenario 1: Multi-Tier Global Web Application

SCENARIO:

You are designing an architecture for a SaaS company that delivers a multi-tenant global web application. The app is expected to serve customers in Europe, North America, and Asia-Pacific. The application consists of a web frontend, a .NET backend API, and a PostgreSQL database.

Requirements:

- 99.99% availability across all regions
- Fast response time and low latency
- Compliance with regional data residency laws
- Seamless failover between regions
- Ability to deploy application updates with zero downtime

Question:

Which combination of services should you include in your design?

A. Azure Front Door, Azure App Service (Premium V3), Azure Database for PostgreSQL – Flexible Server (with zone redundancy)

B. Azure Traffic Manager, Azure Kubernetes Service, Azure PostgreSQL Hyperscale

C. Azure Load Balancer, Azure VM Scale Sets, Azure PostgreSQL Single Server

D. Azure Application Gateway, Azure Functions, Azure Cosmos DB

Correct Answer: A

Walkthrough:

- Azure Front Door provides **global traffic routing**, SSL offloading, and intelligent health probes, which is ideal for high availability and **low-latency** delivery across regions.

- Azure App Service Premium V3 supports **multi-region deployment**, custom domains, deployment slots, and VNET integration.

- Azure Database for PostgreSQL – Flexible Server supports **zone redundancy**, **read replicas**, and **regional failover**, making it suitable for data resiliency and compliance.

Why not B?

AKS and Hyperscale provide great scalability, but AKS requires more management and does not offer zero-downtime upgrades out of the box. Traffic Manager is DNS-based and slower for failover than Front Door.

Why not C?

VM Scale Sets and Load Balancer are IaaS and introduce unnecessary operational complexity. PostgreSQL Single Server lacks redundancy features needed for this SLA.

Why not D?

App Gateway is regional only, not global. Cosmos DB is not PostgreSQL-compatible and might violate data residency laws unless configured with strict partitioning.

Practice Scenario 2: Regulatory-Compliant Data Processing

SCENARIO:

A financial services firm must design a solution to process sensitive transaction data and store it long-term. The system must be compliant with **PCI DSS** and retain logs for **7 years**. The solution must also be cost-efficient and auditable.

Question:

Which components best meet the compliance and long-term retention requirements?

A. Azure SQL Database, Azure Blob Storage with lifecycle rules, Azure Monitor Logs

B. Azure Cosmos DB, Azure File Storage, Event Grid

C. Azure Table Storage, Azure Logic Apps, Azure Data Lake Analytics

D. Azure PostgreSQL, Azure Data Lake Storage Gen2, Azure Monitor with Log Analytics Workspace

---

Correct Answer: D

Walkthrough:

- Azure PostgreSQL is **fully managed**, supports **data encryption**, **audit logging**, and integrates with **Azure AD** and VNET for secure access.
- Data Lake Storage Gen2 is ideal for **long-term retention** and **hierarchical namespace support**, with lifecycle management and granular access control (ACL).
- Log Analytics Workspaces can **store logs for up to 7 years** with configurable retention and are **ISO/PCI DSS compliant**.

Why not A?

Blob Storage is suitable for cold storage but lacks the hierarchical and compliance capabilities of ADLS Gen2. SQL DB is acceptable, but PostgreSQL is better suited for some compliance-specific workloads.

Why not B/C?

Cosmos DB and Table Storage are not ideal for structured transactional data needing relational integrity. Logic Apps and Event Grid are useful for automation but not for audit trail compliance.

Practice Scenario 3: Application Integration with Legacy Systems

SCENARIO:

A manufacturing company is building a new ordering system in Azure. However, it must integrate with an on-premises ERP that only supports SOAP and runs on an internal network. The new system includes an API layer, order database, and batch processing component.

Requirements:

- Secure communication between cloud and on-prem
- Minimal code changes to ERP
- Highly available API endpoints
- Decoupled processing of order events

Question:

Which architecture best satisfies these requirements?

A. Azure Logic Apps with On-Premises Data Gateway, Azure API Management, Azure SQL, Azure Service Bus

B. Azure Functions, Azure ExpressRoute, Azure Cosmos DB, Azure Event Grid

C. Azure API Management with VNET integration, Azure Blob Storage, Azure Event Hubs

D. Azure App Service, Azure Application Gateway, Azure Virtual Network Peering

---

Correct Answer: A

Walkthrough:

- Logic Apps can **integrate with SOAP** using the **On-Premises Data Gateway**, allowing cloud workflows to talk to ERP.
- Azure API Management abstracts the APIs securely with policies and VNET integration.
- Service Bus decouples order processing from database updates or downstream services.

Why not B?

Functions and Event Grid are great, but they cannot directly talk to on-prem systems without tunneling or rewriting legacy logic. ExpressRoute is overkill unless guaranteed bandwidth is needed.

Why not C/D?

Event Hubs is for telemetry ingestion, not order processing. Blob Storage doesn't provide transactional capabilities. Virtual Network Peering only connects VNets, not on-prem resources.

Practice Scenario 4: Secure User Access and Governance

SCENARIO:

A large enterprise needs to enforce strict identity and access policies across its Azure subscriptions. The governance model must include centralized management, role enforcement, and policy compliance across 10+ business units.

Question:

What should you implement to enforce centralized access and governance?

A. Azure Management Groups, Azure Policy, Azure Blueprints, Azure AD PIM

B. Resource Groups, Network Security Groups, Azure Monitor, Azure AD Connect

C. Azure AD B2C, Application Security Groups, Azure Front Door

D. Azure Lighthouse, Azure Functions, Azure DevOps Repos

Correct Answer: A

Walkthrough:

- Management Groups allow for **hierarchical organization** of subscriptions and role-based inheritance.
- Azure Policy and Blueprints enforce **compliance at scale** with reusable governance artifacts.
- Azure AD PIM (Privileged Identity Management) ensures **just-in-time** access and governance of roles.

Why not B?

These are tactical elements. They don't provide enterprise-wide governance or role control.

Why not C?

B2C is for external identity management. ASGs and Front Door deal with networking, not governance.

Why not D?

Lighthouse is for delegated management across tenants, not intra-enterprise governance. Functions and DevOps are unrelated to identity governance.

Exam Strategy Recap from Practice Scenarios

PATTERNS IDENTIFIED:

- Always evaluate **trade-offs** in performance, cost, security, and maintainability

- Read every requirement closely—**availability**, **compliance**, and **latency** often influence the right answer

- Assume Microsoft-recommended best practices unless stated otherwise (e.g., Front Door for global routing, App Service for PaaS)

Design Tips:

- **Availability**: Use multi-region, zone-redundant services

- **Latency**: Use Azure Front Door or Content Delivery Network (CDN)

- **Compliance**: Consider data residency, long-term retention, private endpoints

- **Security**: Use managed identities, RBAC, and network isolation

• **Scalability**: Implement autoscaling, event-driven architecture, and stateless components

---

Summary

PRACTICING SCENARIO-based questions is critical for mastering the AZ-305 exam. Each question should be treated as a real-world design conversation, not a trivia test. By understanding architectural decisions within business, technical, and operational contexts, you prepare not just to pass the exam—but to thrive as an Azure Solutions Architect.

Key Takeaways:

• Focus on business outcomes and constraints

• Eliminate answers that violate clear requirements

• Use Azure-native PaaS wherever possible unless legacy or compliance dictates otherwise

• Understand both tactical services and strategic governance models

• Practice under exam conditions to refine your timing and stress handling

In the next section, we'll discuss **time management strategies** for the exam itself, including how to approach case studies, flag questions, and allocate your time for maximum effectiveness.

Time Management Strategies During the Exam

THE AZ-305 EXAM PRESENTS not only a technical challenge but also a time management one. With approximately 100–120 minutes to answer 40–60 architecturally complex questions, your success hinges on more than just knowledge. Strategic time allocation, mental pacing, and question prioritization are critical. Many candidates fail not because they lack the right answers, but because they mismanage the exam structure—spending too long on case studies, overthinking best-answer scenarios, or running out of time to review flagged questions.

This section provides a thorough guide to managing your time effectively during the exam, from pre-exam preparation to in-exam tactics and post-question review. It includes a breakdown of typical question types, recommended timing, mental endurance techniques, and strategies for maximizing your score even under pressure.

Understand the Exam Structure and Timing Constraints

Element	Typical Count	Estimated Time Allocation	Strategy
Case Studies	1–3	25–35 minutes	Read once thoroughly, then solve
Single/ Multiple Choice	30–40	45–60 minutes	Allocate ~1.5 minutes per question
Drag-and-Drop	3–6	10–15 minutes	Solve last or flag for review
Hot Area Questions	2–4	5–10 minutes	Use elimination, don't overthink
Review and Final Pass	N/A	10–15 minutes	Prioritize flagged/ high-weight

RULE OF THUMB: Allocate 1.5–2 minutes per question, and monitor your progress every 15–20 questions.

Pre-Exam Time Management Preparation

BEFORE THE EXAM BEGINS, you will complete identity verification and read through the exam interface instructions.

Strategies:

- Use the **initial 5-minute buffer** to orient yourself with the interface
- Check keyboard navigation, scratchpad access, and flagging functionality
- Do a quick breathing exercise or meditation to reduce cortisol levels and improve focus

Mental Prep Checklist:

- I am not here to solve everything perfectly—just to **maximize correct answers**
- I will **budget time**, not burn it chasing perfect solutions
- I will flag questions that need reconsideration and move on assertively

---

Managing Case Study Questions

CASE STUDIES SIMULATE real-world scenarios with 3–6 questions per set. Once you leave a case study section, **you cannot return**—this is critical.

Time Allocation: Spend **no more than 10–12 minutes per case study**, regardless of how many questions are involved.

Strategy:

1. **Skim the entire scenario** and note:

    ○ Business goals

    ○ Technical requirements

    ○ Compliance constraints

    ○ Existing architecture (often shown in diagrams or tables)

2. Triage each question based on type:

    ○ **Best fit**: Eliminate clearly wrong options, then choose best based on the scenario

    ○ **True/false**: Treat each statement on its own merit

    ○ **Multiple answers**: Count how many options must be selected (it's usually specified)

3. **Do not over-read.** Focus only on the elements that influence that specific question.

Tip: Use keywords like "must," "required," "ensure," and "not allowed" to identify strict constraints.

Tackling Single and Multiple-Choice Questions

MOST OF YOUR TIME WILL be spent on these. The key is to **treat each question like a mini design challenge**.

Strategy:

- **Read the question first**, then scan the options

- Eliminate answers that:
  - Violate compliance requirements
  - Don't align with Azure best practices
  - Introduce complexity where a native service is available
- If you're stuck, flag and move on—don't waste more than **2 minutes** on a question

Red flags that hint incorrect choices:

- Use of VMs or IaaS where PaaS suffices
- Choosing App Gateway for global routing (instead of Front Door)
- Suggesting SQL MI in a multi-tenant SaaS with per-customer schema

---

Handling Drag-and-Drop and Hot Area Items

THESE ITEMS REQUIRE arranging steps, choosing configuration parameters, or highlighting correct architecture components.

Strategy:

- Solve these in the second half of the exam
- If unsure, eliminate clearly wrong configurations and make an educated guess
- Flag them early and revisit with spare time

Common Drag-and-Drop Topics:

- Steps to implement hybrid identity
- Order of actions to configure VNet peering or site recovery
- Service tier selection based on performance needs

Time-Budgeting Techniques

USE THE 20-40-60-80 rule:

Time Elapsed	Target Progress
20 minutes	Complete 10–15 questions
40 minutes	Reach half of the exam
60 minutes	Case studies completed
80 minutes	All questions answered at least once
Final 20 mins	Review flagged/high-risk questions

This pacing guide helps avoid end-of-exam panic and ensures you reserve time for high-value reviews.

Other Techniques:

- **Pomodoro approach**: Mentally segment the exam into 25-minute focus sprints with 1–2 minutes of recovery (breathing, blinking, stretching)
- **Count backward**: Monitor how many questions remain every 10–15 minutes and recalculate your average available time

---

Flagging and Review Strategy

USE THE **flag feature** for:

- Questions with multiple plausible answers
- Questions where your first guess was rushed

- Questions that are long but not time-sensitive

Do not flag more than 10–12 total questions, or you'll overwhelm your review window.

During review:

- Focus only on flagged questions unless you have excess time
- Prioritize revisiting **case study-type questions** that allow it (some don't)
- Change an answer **only if** you find a clear error in your logic

---

Managing Cognitive Load

THE AZ-305 EXAM CAN feel mentally exhausting. Use micro-strategies to maintain clarity and focus:

- **Blink often** to refresh your eyes
- Breathe in for 4 seconds, hold for 4, exhale for 6 (4–4–6 method)
- Sit in an upright, supported position to reduce fatigue
- Don't reread entire scenarios—skim only the necessary sections
- Mentally label each question: [Easy] / [Hard] / [Maybe] and respond accordingly

---

Prioritizing High-Impact Topics

IF YOU'RE PRESSED FOR time, target questions from **high-weight domains** first:

Domain	Weight
Design Infrastructure Solutions	30–35%
Design Identity, Governance, Monitoring	25–30%
Design Data Storage Solutions	20–25%
Design Business Continuity	10–15%

For example, a question about VM SKUs, VNet peering, or hybrid networking carries more scoring weight than a question about blob lifecycle policies.

If You're Running Out of Time

- PRIORITIZE ANSWERING every question—**never leave any unanswered**
- For multiple-answer questions, **guess conservatively** if time is tight
- Choose answers based on architectural principles:
    - Simplicity > complexity
    - Resilience > single point of failure
    - PaaS > IaaS
    - Secure by default > permissive access

Emergency Triage Plan (Last 10 minutes):

- Answer all unanswered questions (guess if needed)
- Revisit 2–3 high-priority flags
- Skim for obvious errors (e.g., selecting ExpressRoute when VPN was the only choice)

Summary

EFFECTIVE TIME MANAGEMENT during the AZ-305 exam is just as important as your technical knowledge. The exam rewards clarity of thought, decision-making under pressure, and a confident understanding of Azure design patterns. By budgeting your time, recognizing the structure of each question type, and practicing mental pacing, you significantly increase your chances of success.

Key Takeaways:

- Spend no more than 10–12 minutes on case studies
- Average 1.5–2 minutes per question for single-choice items
- Flag strategically, but not excessively
- Use mental markers (Easy/Hard/Maybe) to maintain flow
- Always prioritize high-weight domains
- Maintain energy with intentional breathing and posture resets

In the next section, we'll close the exam preparation journey with a final review checklist and a personalized study plan template to guide your final days before taking the AZ-305 exam.

Final Review Checklist and Study Plan

AS YOUR AZ-305 EXAM approaches, the final days of preparation are critical for consolidating knowledge, reinforcing weak areas, and mentally preparing to approach the exam with confidence and clarity. By this stage, you should already have a solid understanding of Azure architecture, core services, design principles, and governance strategies. What remains is systematic revision, focused practice, and a clearly defined game plan.

This section presents a structured **final review checklist** and a **7-day study plan** tailored for optimal last-mile exam readiness. It includes review areas by topic, last-minute high-yield concepts, and mindset techniques to maintain focus and reduce anxiety before test day.

Final 7-Day Study Plan Overview

Day	Focus Area	Activities
1	Identity & Governance	RBAC, Azure AD, Policies, Blueprints, PIM
2	Storage Design	Account types, redundancy, access, lifecycle, Cosmos vs SQL
3	Business Continuity	RPO/RTO, Azure Backup, ASR, availability sets vs zones
4	Infrastructure Design	VNets, ExpressRoute, hybrid, VMSS, AKS, PaaS patterns
5	Application Architecture & Monitoring	API Management, Logic Apps, Functions, App Insights, event patterns
6	Case Study Simulation & Practice Questions	Practice 3–4 full case studies + review answers
7	Quick Revision + Relaxation	Flashcards, review notes, light reading, system prep

EACH DAY SHOULD INCLUDE **2–3 hours of focused review**, with breaks and practice questions distributed in 25–30 minute cycles.

Final Review Checklist by Exam Domain

1. Design Identity, Governance, and Monitoring Solutions

- UNDERSTAND TENANT vs subscription vs resource group hierarchy
- Know how to assign and enforce **RBAC** using least-privilege
- Differentiate between **Azure Policy**, **Blueprints**, and **Locks**
- Use **Management Groups** for governance at scale
- Configure **Privileged Identity Management (PIM)** and **Conditional Access**
- Monitor with **Azure Monitor**, **Log Analytics**, **Activity Logs**, and **Diagnostic Settings**
- Track metrics with **KQL queries** and configure **alerts**

Example Question:

How would you enforce that all VMs in a subscription are encrypted and tagged for billing?

Answer: Use Azure Policy assignment + initiative with effects auditIfNotExists and modify.

---

2. Design Data Storage Solutions

- CHOOSE BETWEEN **Standard** and **Premium** storage
- Understand **Geo-redundant** (GRS), **Zone-redundant** (ZRS), and **Locally redundant** (LRS)

- Secure storage with **SAS tokens, private endpoints, firewalls,** and **RBAC**
- Compare use cases: **Blob vs File vs Queue vs Table**
- Know when to use **Cosmos DB** (multi-model, multi-region, global distribution)
- Implement **retention policies** and **immutability (WORM)** on containers
- Design archival strategies using **Blob tiers**: hot, cool, archive

Example Question:

What's the best solution for audit log storage with immutability and 7-year retention?

Answer: Azure Blob Storage with immutable blob policy and Archive tier.

---

3. Design Business Continuity and Disaster Recovery Solutions

- DEFINE AND CALCULATE **RPO (Recovery Point Objective)** and **RTO (Recovery Time Objective)**
- Use **Availability Zones** vs **Availability Sets** appropriately
- Plan for **cross-region failover** using **Azure Site Recovery (ASR)**
- Implement **Azure Backup** with appropriate vault and policy configurations
- Architect multi-region deployments using **Traffic Manager** or **Front Door**
- Understand **Active-Active** and **Active-Passive** patterns

Example Question:

Which combination ensures automatic failover and minimum downtime for an e-commerce backend?

Answer: Azure Front Door + multi-region App Service deployment with Geo-redundant DB.

---

4. Design Infrastructure Solutions

- BUILD NETWORK TOPOLOGY using **hub-and-spoke**, **Virtual WAN**, and **VNet peering**
- Configure **ExpressRoute**, **VPN Gateway**, and **private endpoints**
- Know when to use **App Service**, **AKS**, **Functions**, or **VMSS**
- Apply **autoscaling**, **load balancing**, and **custom domains/SSL**
- Secure traffic using **NSGs**, **ASGs**, and **Azure Firewall**
- Understand compute SKUs and cost implications

Example Question:

Which service combination offers high-scale compute with auto-patching and minimal ops overhead?

Answer: Azure App Service Premium with autoscale and staging slots.

---

5. Design Application Architecture and Integration

- USE **Event Grid**, **Service Bus**, **Event Hubs** based on latency, throughput, and order needs

- Expose and protect APIs with **API Management** + rate limiting and OAuth
- Integrate workflows using **Logic Apps**, **Functions**, and **Durable Functions**
- Implement **microservices** with **AKS** and service mesh
- Set up **Application Insights** and **distributed tracing**
- Instrument applications for **custom events**, **exceptions**, and **availability tests**

Example Question:

How would you orchestrate a 3-step order processing flow with error compensation?

Answer: Durable Functions with chained activities and retry policies.

Additional Final Review Tools

Flashcard Concepts to Master:

- IDENTITY: MFA, CONDITIONAL Access, PIM, B2B/B2C
- Networking: DNS, VNet, NSG, UDR, ASG, Firewall
- Storage: Lifecycle, replication types, secured access
- Compute: VMSS, autoscale, App Service plans
- Resiliency: Front Door, ZRS, GRS, availability zones
- Messaging: Event Grid vs Service Bus vs Event Hub

- Governance: Policy, Blueprints, Resource Locks
- Monitoring: KQL, Alerts, Application Map, Dashboards

Memory Hooks and Short Mnemonics:

- **"PIRATE"** for Resiliency: **P**eering, **I**ntegration, **R**edundancy, **A**vailability Zones, **T**raffic Manager, **E**xpressRoute
- **"3 R's"** for Continuity: **RPO, RTO, Redundancy**

Before the Exam Day: Personal Prep Checklist

- I HAVE REVIEWED the exam objectives in the Microsoft official skills outline
- I have completed at least 2 full-length practice exams
- I've memorized the key SKUs, service limits, and access tiers
- I know how to design for compliance (e.g., GDPR, PCI, ISO 27001)
- My test environment (camera, microphone, quiet space) is set up for online proctoring
- I've reviewed my ID and Pearson VUE account details
- I've backed up my notes to OneNote, PDF, or a Notion board

Final Day Preparation (Day Before Exam)

- **Morning:** Review key services, high-value tables, case studies
- **Afternoon:** Light practice with 10–15 sample questions, then stop

- **Evening:** Eat light, hydrate, avoid screen fatigue
- **Night:** Ensure at least 7–8 hours of sleep. Don't cram.

Mental Strategy for Test Day

- TRUST YOUR INSTINCTS: First answer is often correct
- Manage your pace: No more than 2 minutes per standard question
- Flag smartly: Come back to complex items if time permits
- Read carefully: Many traps are in modifiers like "most cost-effective" or "must comply"
- Breathe: Inhale slowly, exhale longer to slow heart rate and stay calm

Summary

THE FINAL STRETCH OF AZ-305 preparation is about confidence, consolidation, and strategy. By methodically reviewing the domains, practicing focused scenario questions, and mentally preparing for exam dynamics, you set yourself up for success. This is not just about passing an exam—it's about proving your ability to architect real solutions that meet business, compliance, and technical requirements.

Final Thoughts:

- Review deliberately—not exhaustively
- Prioritize comprehension over memorization
- Balance technical study with mindset and rest

- Walk into the exam room not just as a candidate, but as a cloud architect ready to lead

In the next chapter, you'll find supplementary resources, a glossary of essential terms, and sample architectural blueprints to reinforce your AZ-305 journey beyond the exam.

Chapter 8: Appendices

Glossary of Terms

UNDERSTANDING THE TERMINOLOGY used throughout Azure's architecture, services, and the AZ-305 exam objectives is essential for mastering both the certification and real-world design scenarios. This glossary provides clear, concise definitions of the most commonly referenced terms and acronyms in cloud solution architecture, with a focus on Azure-specific concepts. These definitions are written to provide quick recall and are organized alphabetically for ease of use during your review process.

Access Control (IAM):

Role-based system used to manage who has access to Azure resources, what they can do with those resources, and what areas they can access.

Active Directory (Azure AD):

Microsoft's cloud-based identity and access management service. Used for managing users, groups, and access to resources. It supports SSO, MFA, conditional access, and integration with on-premises AD.

Application Gateway:

A Layer 7 (application layer) load balancer that enables routing based on URL paths and supports Web Application Firewall (WAF) for security.

Application Insights:

Part of Azure Monitor, this tool collects telemetry from apps for monitoring performance, usage, and diagnostics, supporting distributed tracing and live metrics.

Application Security Group (ASG):

Logical groupings of VMs in the same virtual network, enabling NSG rules to be applied at scale to workloads.

App Service (Web Apps):

PaaS offering for hosting web applications, REST APIs, and mobile backends with built-in autoscaling, SSL, deployment slots, and VNET integration.

Azure Arc:

Extends Azure management and services to any infrastructure, including on-premises, multi-cloud, and edge environments.

Azure Blueprints:

A declarative way to orchestrate the deployment of various resource templates and policies, ensuring compliance and consistency across environments.

Azure CLI:

Command-line tool for managing Azure resources. Often used in scripting and automation workflows.

Azure Cosmos DB:

Globally distributed, multi-model NoSQL database with guaranteed single-digit millisecond response times, high availability, and elastic scalability.

Azure DevOps:

A suite of tools for CI/CD pipelines, version control, testing, and project management tailored for enterprise development workflows.

Azure DNS:

Azure-hosted DNS domain services that provide name resolution for resources, with integration to Azure networking.

Azure Files:

Fully managed file shares in the cloud, accessible via SMB and NFS protocols, supporting on-premises access with Azure File Sync.

Azure Firewall:

Stateful firewall-as-a-service with built-in high availability, unrestricted cloud scalability, and centralized logging.

Azure Front Door:

Global application delivery service that offers SSL termination, path-based routing, web application acceleration, and global load balancing.

Azure Key Vault:

Securely stores secrets, keys, and certificates with controlled access and logging capabilities. Integrated with most Azure services.

Azure Kubernetes Service (AKS):

Managed Kubernetes container orchestration service that automates deployment, scaling, and operations of Kubernetes clusters.

Azure Load Balancer:

Provides Layer 4 (TCP/UDP) load balancing across virtual machines, supports inbound NAT rules, and health probes.

Azure Monitor:

Unified monitoring solution for collecting, analyzing, and acting on telemetry from cloud and on-premise environments.

Azure Policy:

Enables the creation and assignment of rules to enforce resource compliance across subscriptions or resource groups.

Azure Private Link:

Provides private connectivity from virtual networks to Azure PaaS, customer-owned, or Microsoft partner services.

Azure Resource Manager (ARM):

Azure's deployment and management service. Allows infrastructure to be defined via templates (ARM templates), managed as a single entity.

Azure Site Recovery (ASR):

Disaster recovery service that orchestrates replication, failover, and recovery of workloads between regions or from on-premises to Azure.

Azure SQL Database:

Managed relational database service with high availability, backup, and scaling capabilities. Offers Hyperscale and Serverless tiers.

Azure Storage Account:

Logical namespace that gives access to storage services like Blob, Table, Queue, and File services with encryption and replication options.

Azure Virtual Network (VNet):

Fundamental building block for private networking in Azure, enabling communication between Azure resources, on-premises, and the internet.

Azure Virtual WAN:

Networking service that provides optimized, automated, and scalable branch connectivity to Azure and through Azure.

Availability Set:

Provides redundancy by distributing VMs across fault and update domains, ensuring high availability during maintenance events.

Availability Zone:

Physically separate locations within an Azure region, each with independent power, cooling, and networking for resiliency.

Bicep:

A domain-specific language (DSL) for deploying Azure resources declaratively. Simplifies authoring compared to JSON-based ARM templates.

Bring Your Own IP (BYOIP):

Allows organizations to use their existing public IP addresses within Azure.

Business Continuity and Disaster Recovery (BCDR):

Strategies and services to ensure applications continue during planned or unplanned outages and meet SLA and compliance requirements.

Case Study:

Scenario-based question format in AZ-305 that presents a business problem and requires solution design based on constraints and goals.

Content Delivery Network (CDN):

Globally distributed servers that cache and serve content to users from the nearest edge node, reducing latency.

Conditional Access:

Azure AD feature allowing access policies based on conditions like user risk, device compliance, location, and more.

Container Instance (ACI):

Serverless container solution that allows for fast deployment and scaling of single-container apps without managing infrastructure.

Cross-Origin Resource Sharing (CORS):

Mechanism that allows restricted resources on a web page to be requested from another domain outside the domain from which the resource originated.

Customer Lockbox:

Ensures that Microsoft support engineers can only access your content with explicit approval.

Data Loss Prevention (DLP):

Policies to prevent sensitive information from being improperly shared or leaked within or outside the organization.

Data Residency:

Requirement that customer data be stored within a specific geographic region due to legal, regulatory, or compliance rules.

Dead-letter Queue (DLQ):

Queue used to hold messages that cannot be delivered or processed successfully. Common in Service Bus and Event Grid.

Durable Functions:

Extension of Azure Functions enabling stateful orchestrations and long-running workflows using code.

Elasticity:

Ability of cloud resources to scale automatically in or out based on demand.

ExpressRoute:

Private, dedicated network connection from on-premises infrastructure to Azure, bypassing the public internet for improved security and reliability.

Federation:

Process of establishing trust between two identity providers to allow users to authenticate across organizational boundaries.

Geo-Replication:

Replication of data to another Azure region for high availability and disaster recovery.

Hybrid Cloud:

Architecture that combines on-premises datacenters with public cloud resources to create a unified, flexible environment.

Immutable Blob Storage:

Feature that makes blobs write-once, read-many (WORM), ensuring they cannot be modified or deleted for a specified retention period.

Infrastructure as Code (IaC):

Managing and provisioning infrastructure through machine-readable definition files instead of manual processes.

Load Balancing Rules:

Configurations in Azure Load Balancer that map frontend IP and port to backend pool and port.

Managed Identity:

Azure AD-based identity automatically assigned to Azure resources to securely access other services without credentials.

Management Group:

Hierarchy level above subscription used for applying policies and RBAC at scale.

Multi-Factor Authentication (MFA):

Security mechanism requiring two or more forms of verification for user sign-in.

Network Security Group (NSG):

Contains security rules that allow or deny network traffic to Azure resources in a virtual network.

Peering:

Connects two VNets allowing resources in them to communicate with low latency and high bandwidth without gateways.

Policy Initiative:

A collection of Azure Policies grouped to enforce multiple requirements together as one package.

PaaS (Platform as a Service):

Cloud computing model that delivers hardware and software tools over the internet, typically used for application development.

Queue Storage:

Service for storing large numbers of messages that can be accessed from anywhere using authenticated calls.

Recovery Point Objective (RPO):

Maximum acceptable amount of data loss measured in time.

Recovery Time Objective (RTO):

Maximum acceptable amount of time an application can be down after a failure.

Resource Group:

Container that holds related Azure resources and defines a scope for management and access control.

Role-Based Access Control (RBAC):

System for managing permissions by assigning roles to users, groups, and applications at different scopes.

Service Bus:

Enterprise message broker with support for queues, topics, sessions, and transactions.

Service Principal:

Security identity used by applications or services to access Azure resources.

Shared Access Signature (SAS):

URI that grants restricted access to Azure Storage resources without exposing the account key.

Storage Tiering:

Automatic movement of data between storage tiers (hot, cool, archive) based on usage or rules.

Subscription:

Logical container for billing and resource management in Azure. Belongs to an Azure AD tenant.

Tagging:

Adding metadata to Azure resources for classification, billing, and automation purposes.

Terraform:

Open-source IaC tool used to define and provision Azure infrastructure via a declarative language.

Throughput Unit (TU):

Unit of capacity in Azure Event Hubs determining ingress/egress limits.

Traffic Manager:

DNS-based global traffic distribution service that routes clients to the best performing or closest endpoint.

Virtual Machine Scale Set (VMSS):

Group of identical, load-balanced VMs that auto-scale in response to demand or schedule.

VNET Integration:

Allows an Azure service like App Service or Functions to connect securely to resources inside a VNet.

Vulnerability Assessment:

Analysis tool used to scan databases or systems for security risks, compliance gaps, or misconfigurations.

Summary

THIS GLOSSARY IS DESIGNED as a quick-reference guide to decode and clarify terminology frequently encountered on the AZ-305 exam and in real-world Azure architecture. Mastery of these terms will not only boost exam performance but also enable you to think and communicate like a cloud architect. In the following sections, we'll share curated learning resources, practical project samples, and technical references to further strengthen your expertise.

Resources for Further Learning

A SUCCESSFUL AZURE Solutions Architect doesn't stop learning after passing the AZ-305 exam. As the cloud evolves, so too must your knowledge. Whether your goal is deepening your expertise, maintaining certifications, or preparing for your next architectural project, having the right resources is crucial.

This section curates a comprehensive, categorized list of official documentation, Microsoft Learn paths, architectural guides, books, GitHub repositories, certifications, and community platforms that support continuous Azure learning. These resources will help you stay current, solve real-world challenges, and architect scalable, secure, and cost-effective solutions across cloud environments.

Official Microsoft Resources

1. MICROSOFT LEARN:

- **AZ-305 Learning Path:**

https://learn.microsoft.com/en-us/training/paths/design-infrastructure-solutions-microsoft-azure/

  - Covers all domains: identity, storage, continuity, networking, and governance.
  - Includes interactive labs and knowledge checks.

- **Architecting Microsoft Azure Solutions Collection:**

https://learn.microsoft.com/en-us/azure/architecture/

  - Microsoft's architecture center with guides, decision trees, and best practices.

- Contains real-world reference architectures with diagrams and templates.

- **Azure Well-Architected Framework:**

https://learn.microsoft.com/en-us/azure/architecture/framework/

- A structured approach to evaluate and improve your architecture using five pillars:
  - Reliability
  - Cost Optimization
  - Operational Excellence
  - Performance Efficiency
  - Security

2. Microsoft Documentation Hubs:

- **Azure Services Index:**

https://learn.microsoft.com/en-us/azure/

- Master index for all Azure services, organized by category.

- **Azure CLI Reference:**

https://learn.microsoft.com/en-us/cli/azure/reference-index

- Syntax, flags, and examples for automating resource management.

- **Azure REST API Reference:**

https://learn.microsoft.com/en-us/rest/api/azure/

 ○ RESTful endpoints for scripting or programmatic access to Azure services.

- **Azure Security Documentation:**

https://learn.microsoft.com/en-us/security/azure-security/

 ○ Covers encryption, identity, compliance, threat protection, and governance.

Microsoft Certification Ecosystem

MICROSOFT CERTIFICATIONS Roadmap:

https://learn.microsoft.com/en-us/certifications/

Explore other paths beyond AZ-305:

- **AZ-104**: Azure Administrator Associate
- **AZ-400**: DevOps Engineer Expert
- **SC-100**: Cybersecurity Architect Expert
- **AZ-700**: Azure Network Engineer Associate
- **DP-203**: Data Engineering on Microsoft Azure
- **AI-102**: Designing and Implementing Azure AI Solutions

Microsoft Learn Sandbox:

- Provides free Azure credits for interactive labs:

https://learn.microsoft.com/en-us/training/sandbox/

Architecture and Design Repositories

1. AZURE ARCHITECTURE Center:

- **Reference Architectures:**

https://learn.microsoft.com/en-us/azure/architecture/reference-architectures/

  - Pre-built, production-ready blueprints for common workloads (e.g., multi-region web apps, CI/CD pipelines, SAP on Azure)

- **Design Patterns:**

https://learn.microsoft.com/en-us/azure/architecture/patterns/

  - Proven design patterns like retry, throttling, circuit breaker, CQRS, event sourcing

- **Industry Solutions:**

https://learn.microsoft.com/en-us/azure/industry/

  - Architecture guidance tailored to healthcare, finance, manufacturing, government, etc.

2. Azure Quickstart Templates:

https://github.com/Azure/azure-quickstart-templates

- Community-maintained collection of ARM and Bicep templates.
- Useful for provisioning complete architectures in minutes.

3. Azure Bicep Examples:

https://github.com/Azure/bicep

• Contains modular Bicep files, examples, and CI/CD-ready configurations.

• Helps reinforce IaC practices using native Azure tooling.

Books and Learning Guides

RECOMMENDED BOOKS:

• *Exam Ref AZ-305 Designing Microsoft Azure Infrastructure Solutions*

By Ashish Agrawal, David Rendon

(Microsoft Press) – Exam-focused preparation guide with case studies and review questions.

• *Azure for Architects (O'Reilly)*

By Ritesh Modi

– Deep dives into real-world design scenarios and architecture diagrams.

• *Designing Distributed Systems* by Brendan Burns

– Kubernetes-centric design book by one of the co-founders of AKS.

• *Cloud Design Patterns* (Microsoft eBook)

– Free downloadable PDF covering 24 design patterns in Azure-based applications.

• *Azure Strategy and Implementation Guide*

By Jack Lee, Peter De Tender, Greg Leonardo

– Focused on enterprise cloud adoption strategies and architecture practices.

Labs, Sandboxes, and Simulators

1. AZURE HANDS-ON LABS:

https://www.microsoft.com/handsonlabs

- Browser-based labs that let you explore Azure services without needing a subscription.

2. GitHub – Azure Architecture Labs:

https://github.com/mspnp

- Projects covering AKS, Cosmos DB, Serverless, Functions, Governance, and CI/CD.

3. Microsoft Azure DevOps Generator:

https://azuredevopsdemogenerator.azurewebsites.net/

- Quickly deploy complete DevOps pipelines for various scenarios.

Community Resources and Forums

1. MICROSOFT Q&A:

https://learn.microsoft.com/en-us/answers/products/

- Official support and discussion forum for Azure products.

2. Tech Community:

https://techcommunity.microsoft.com/t5/azure/ct-p/Azure

- Blogs, webinars, and product updates from Azure engineers.

3. Reddit:

- r/AZURE
- r/AzureCertification

Community-driven discussions, success stories, tips, and troubleshooting.

4. Stack Overflow:

- Rich source of real-world problems, error resolution, and developer interaction.

5. YouTube Channels:

- Microsoft Azure (official)
- John Savill's Technical Training
- CloudAcademy
- FreeCodeCamp Azure Playlists

Tools and Portals

1. AZURE PRICING CALCULATOR:

https://azure.microsoft.com/en-us/pricing/calculator/

- Estimate monthly costs for any Azure workload.

2. Azure Advisor:

https://portal.azure.com[1] > Advisor

1. https://portal.azure.com/

- Personalized recommendations to optimize cost, performance, reliability, and security.

3. Azure Migrate:

https://learn.microsoft.com/en-us/azure/migrate/

- Tools for assessing and migrating workloads to Azure.

4. Microsoft Compliance Manager:

https://compliance.microsoft.com[2]

- Monitor compliance with regulatory standards (HIPAA, GDPR, ISO 27001, etc.)

5. Cloud Adoption Framework:

https://learn.microsoft.com/en-us/azure/cloud-adoption-framework/

- Strategic guidance and tooling for enterprise cloud transformation.

Continuing Professional Development

- SUBSCRIBE TO **Azure Updates**:

https://azure.microsoft.com/en-us/updates/

- Attend **Microsoft Ignite**, **Build**, and regional **Azure Bootcamps**
- Join a **Microsoft Azure Meetup Group** near you
- Track certification renewal requirements and use free **renewal assessments** on Microsoft Learn

---

2. https://compliance.microsoft.com/

Summary

THE RESOURCES LISTED here serve as a launchpad for continued growth in Azure architecture beyond AZ-305. Whether you're preparing for advanced certifications, designing complex solutions, or leading enterprise cloud transformations, these tools will support your ongoing development.

Next Steps:

- Create your personal knowledge base in Notion, Obsidian, or OneNote
- Schedule time each week to review new Azure announcements
- Follow Microsoft MVPs and cloud experts on LinkedIn or X (formerly Twitter)
- Continue building—projects are the best teachers

In the next section, you'll find sample project ideas and real-world code snippets that reinforce the patterns, services, and strategies covered throughout the book.

Sample Projects and Code Snippets

ONE OF THE MOST EFFECTIVE ways to solidify your understanding of Azure architecture principles and prepare for real-world implementation is to build practical solutions that simulate business-critical scenarios. This section offers a comprehensive collection of sample project ideas along with architectural guidance, deployment tools, and code snippets in Bicep, ARM, Terraform, CLI, and PowerShell. These projects are aligned with AZ-305 exam domains and are designed to reinforce architectural decisions involving compute, storage, identity, networking, governance, monitoring, and disaster recovery.

Project 1: Multi-Tier Web Application with High Availability

SCENARIO:

Design and deploy a scalable, fault-tolerant web application architecture using Azure services that supports global access and zero downtime deployments.

Architecture Includes:

- Azure Front Door (global routing)
- Azure App Service with deployment slots (blue/green deployments)
- Azure SQL Database (zone-redundant)
- Azure Monitor with Application Insights
- Azure Key Vault for storing secrets

Bicep Sample:

```
resource appServicePlan 'Microsoft.Web/serverfarms@2022-03-01' = {
name: 'asp-global-web'
location: resourceGroup().location
sku: {
name: 'P1v3'
```

```
tier: 'PremiumV3'
}
properties: {
reserved: false
}
}
resource app 'Microsoft.Web/sites@2022-03-01' = {
name: 'webfrontend'
location: resourceGroup().location
properties: {
serverFarmId: appServicePlan.id
siteConfig: {
alwaysOn: true
}
}
}
```

Key Concepts Reinforced:

- Zone redundancy
- Blue/green deployment strategy
- Role separation for admin vs devs

- Metrics and logs aggregation

Project 2: Secure Hybrid Connectivity with On-Prem Integration

SCENARIO:

Extend your on-premises network into Azure securely to support hybrid workloads like database mirroring, backup replication, and federated identity.

Architecture Includes:

- Azure VPN Gateway (route-based)
- On-prem router emulator (e.g., pfSense VM)
- Azure Bastion for secure VM management
- Azure Key Vault and RBAC
- Azure Policy for enforcing tagging and encryption

Azure CLI Snippet:

az network vnet create \

—name hub-vnet \

—resource-group rg-hybrid \

—address-prefix 10.0.0.0/16 \

—subnet-name GatewaySubnet \

—subnet-prefix 10.0.0.0/24

az network vpn-gateway create \

—resource-group rg-hybrid \

—name hub-vpn \

—vnet hub-vnet \

—public-ip-address hub-vpn-ip \

—sku VpnGw1 \

—gateway-type Vpn \

—vpn-type RouteBased

Key Concepts Reinforced:

- Hybrid identity with Azure AD Connect
- VPN Gateway configuration and routing
- Centralized bastion access
- Enforcing governance via policy

Project 3: Event-Driven Serverless Architecture

SCENARIO:

Build a serverless image processing pipeline triggered by Blob Storage uploads, with downstream operations and notifications.

Architecture Includes:

- Azure Blob Storage (container with Event Grid)
- Azure Function (image processing logic)
- Azure Service Bus Queue (decoupled processing)

- Azure Logic App (notification workflow)

Function Trigger Code (JavaScript):

```
module.exports = async function (context, myBlob) {
context.log("Blob processed:", context.bindingData.blobTrigger);
// Placeholder: Image resize, metadata extraction
};
```

Event Subscription (CLI):

```
az eventgrid event-subscription create \
—name image-upload-sub \
—source-resource-id /subscriptions/xxx/resourceGroups/rg-app/providers/Microsoft.Storage/storageAccounts/myblobstore \
—endpoint-type azurefunction \
—endpoint /subscriptions/xxx/resourceGroups/rg-app/providers/Microsoft.Web/sites/imgfunc/functions/ProcessImage
```

Key Concepts Reinforced:

- Event Grid vs Service Bus integration
- Stateless compute via Functions
- Queue-based load leveling
- Cost optimization using consumption plan

Project 4: Application Monitoring with Custom Alerts

SCENARIO:

Instrument an existing application with telemetry, build custom queries, set up smart alerts, and visualize performance trends.

Architecture Includes:

- Azure Monitor and Application Insights
- Custom events, metrics, and logging
- Kusto Query Language (KQL)
- Alert rules + Action Groups
- Workbook dashboard

KQL Sample – High Latency Calls:

```
requests
| where duration > 500
| summarize avg(duration) by name, bin(timestamp, 5m)
| order by avg_duration desc
```

PowerShell Alert Creation:

```
New-AzMetricAlertRuleV2 -ResourceGroupName "rg-app" `
-Name "HighLatencyAlert" `
-Location "westeurope" `
```

-TargetResourceId "/subscriptions/.../providers/microsoft.insights/components/appinsights" `

-WindowSize 00:05:00 `

-Frequency 00:01:00 `

-Severity 2 `

-Criteria @(New-AzMetricAlertRuleV2Criteria -MetricName "Request Duration" -Operator GreaterThan -Threshold 500)

Key Concepts Reinforced:

- Alerting thresholds and granularity
- Combining logs and metrics
- Visualizations for leadership or NOC teams
- Proactive monitoring

Project 5: Resilient Multiregion API Deployment

SCENARIO:

Deploy a stateless API across two Azure regions with automatic failover and distributed traffic control.

Architecture Includes:

- Azure API Management (multi-region)
- Azure App Service with staging slots
- Azure Traffic Manager (priority routing)
- Cosmos DB with multi-region writes

- Azure Front Door (optional layer 7 global routing)

Terraform Snippet for Traffic Manager:

```
resource "azurerm_traffic_manager_profile" "api_tm" {
name = "api-global-profile"
resource_group_name = azurerm_resource_group.main.name
location = "global"
traffic_routing_method = "Priority"
dns_config {
relative_name = "api-global"
ttl = 30
}
monitor_config {
protocol = "HTTP"
port = 80
path = "/health"
}
}
```

Key Concepts Reinforced:

- Priority vs performance-based routing
- Geo-distribution of Cosmos DB

- Health probes and failover
- Canary deployment via slots

Project 6: Cost Governance and Budgeting System

SCENARIO:

Implement a cost visibility and alerting strategy across a multi-subscription Azure estate.

Architecture Includes:

- Azure Cost Management + Budgets
- Azure Policy to restrict expensive SKUs
- Management Groups for scope enforcement
- Tagging for cost center attribution
- Logic App for budget threshold email alerts

Policy Sample (Deny Premium SKUs):

```
{
"if": {
"allOf": [
{
"field": "sku.name",
"equals": "Premium"
},
```

```
{
"field": "type",
"equals": "Microsoft.Web/serverfarms"
}
]
},
"then": {
"effect": "deny"
}
}
```

Key Concepts Reinforced:

- Budget thresholds and automation
- Enforcing compliance via policy
- Cost tagging and reporting
- Centralized governance via management groups

Summary

THESE SAMPLE PROJECTS represent practical, exam-aligned Azure architecture implementations that reinforce the theoretical principles covered throughout this guide. By deploying even a subset of these solutions, you'll not only prepare for AZ-305 but also build a portfolio of real-world experience that aligns with the demands of enterprise cloud roles.

Recommended Next Steps:

- Deploy each project in a sandbox or Azure free tier
- Use Git to version-control your infrastructure (IaC)
- Share your architectures on GitHub or in blog posts to showcase your learning
- Expand complexity over time (e.g., add CI/CD, integrate Azure DevOps, or refactor to microservices)

In the next appendix, we provide an API reference guide outlining commonly used endpoints, parameters, and authentication practices for integrating Azure services programmatically.

API Reference Guide

APIS ARE A FUNDAMENTAL aspect of working with Azure at an architectural level. Whether you're automating deployments, integrating services, or building cloud-native applications, knowing how to interact with Azure through its REST APIs and SDKs is essential. This section serves as a detailed reference guide to help you use Azure's API ecosystem effectively. It includes information about core Azure REST APIs, SDK usage patterns, authentication strategies, endpoint structures, common headers, error handling, and service-specific examples.

This reference is intended for architects who need to design extensible systems, DevOps engineers implementing infrastructure as code, and developers building integrations or automation workflows using programmatic interfaces.

Core API Concepts

AZURE OFFERS SEVERAL types of APIs:

- **Azure REST APIs** – Low-level HTTP-based APIs that enable direct access to management operations.
- **SDKs (Azure SDK for .NET, JavaScript, Python, etc.)** – High-level libraries that abstract REST APIs and simplify integration.
- **Azure CLI & PowerShell** – Scripting interfaces that internally call REST APIs but offer human-readable syntax.

Understanding how to structure and authenticate requests, handle responses, and manage tokens is vital for any use case that requires code-based interaction.

Authentication Overview

AZURE APIS USE **Azure Active Directory (Azure AD)** for securing access through OAuth 2.0.

Steps to authenticate:

1. Register an app in Azure AD (via portal or CLI)
2. Assign API permissions (e.g., user_impersonation)
3. Obtain an access token using client credentials or authorization code flow
4. Include the token in the Authorization header when calling the API

Example Token Request (Client Credentials Grant):

POST https://login.microsoftonline.com/{tenant-id}/oauth2/v2.0/token

Content-Type: application/x-www-form-urlencoded

client_id={client-id}

&scope=https://management.azure.com/.default

&client_secret={client-secret}

&grant_type=client_credentials

Accessing APIs:

GET https://management.azure.com/subscriptions/{subscriptionId}/resources?api-version=2022-01-01

Authorization: Bearer {access_token}

Common Request Headers

Header	Description
Authorization	Bearer {access_token}
Content-Type	Typically application/json
x-ms-client-request-id	Unique GUID per request (optional)
x-ms-correlation-request-id	For distributed tracing (optional)
Accept	application/json

Common Management API Endpoints

AZURE MANAGEMENT APIS use the base URI:

https://management.azure.com/

List all resource groups:

GET
/SUBSCRIPTIONS/{subscriptionId}/resourcegroups?api-version=202

Get a specific resource:

GET
/SUBSCRIPTIONS/{subscriptionId}/resourceGroups/{resourceGroupN

Create a virtual network:

PUT
/SUBSCRIPTIONS/{subscriptionId}/resourceGroups/{resourceGroupN
Microsoft.Network/
virtualNetworks/{vnetName}?api-version=2022-01-01

```
{
"location": "eastus",
"properties": {
"addressSpace": {
"addressPrefixes": ["10.0.0.0/16"]
},
"subnets": [{
"name": "default",
"properties": {
"addressPrefix": "10.0.0.0/24"
}
}]
}
```

}

Delete a resource group:

DELETE
/SUBSCRIPTIONS/{subscriptionId}/resourcegroups/{resourceGroupNa

Azure Resource Manager (ARM) APIs

ARM APIS SUPPORT **idempotent deployments** and are used for:

- Deploying templates (ARM or Bicep)
- Managing deployments
- Querying resource health and states

Example: Deploy an ARM template:

```
PUT
/subscriptions/{subscriptionId}/resourcegroups/{resourceGroupName}/pr
Microsoft.Resources/
deployments/{deploymentName}?api-version=2021-04-01

{

"properties": {

"mode": "Incremental",

"template": { /* ARM Template JSON */ },

"parameters": { /* Parameter values */ }

}

}
```

Response includes:

- provisioningState
- timestamp
- correlationId for diagnostics

Azure Monitor and Log Analytics API

THESE APIS ALLOW YOU to query logs, retrieve metrics, and create alert rules.

Query Logs (KQL):

POST /subscriptions/{subscriptionId}/resourceGroups/{resourceGroupName}/p Microsoft.OperationalInsights/ workspaces/{workspaceName}/query?api-version=2021-12-01-preview

{

"query": "Heartbeat | summarize count() by bin(TimeGenerated, 1h)"

}

Response:

{

"tables": [

{

"columns": [{ "name": "TimeGenerated", "type": "datetime" }, ...],

"rows": [["2024-12-01T00:00:00Z", 102], ...]

}

]

}

Get Azure Metrics:

GET
/subscriptions/{subscriptionId}/resourceGroups/{rg}/providers/
Microsoft.Compute/virtualMachines/{vm}/providers/
microsoft.insights/metrics?metricnames=Percentage
CPU&timespan=PT1H&interval=PT5M&aggregation=Average&api-v

Azure Key Vault API

USED TO PROGRAMMATICALLY retrieve or store secrets, keys, and certificates.

Get a secret:

GET https://{vault-name}.vault.azure.net/secrets/{secret-name}?api-version=7.4

Authorization: Bearer {token}

Create/Update a secret:

PUT https://{vault-name}.vault.azure.net/secrets/db-password?api-version=7.4

{

"value": "P@ssw0rd123"

}

Azure Cosmos DB REST API

USED FOR DIRECT INTERACTION with Cosmos DB collections and documents. Cosmos uses **custom headers and a master key** instead of OAuth.

Sample Request – Query Documents:

```
POST https://{account}.documents.azure.com/dbs/{db}/colls/{coll}/docs

x-ms-date: {utc-date}

x-ms-version: 2018-12-31

x-ms-documentdb-isquery: true

Authorization: {auth-header}

{

"query": "SELECT * FROM c"

}
```

Authentication: Uses HMAC signature created from master key.

Error Handling and Response Codes

AZURE APIS RETURN STANDARD HTTP status codes:

Status Code	Meaning
200 OK	Request successful
201 Created	Resource successfully created
202 Accepted	Request accepted for async execution
204 No Content	Request succeeded, no content
400 Bad Request	Input validation failed
401 Unauthorized	Invalid or missing token
403 Forbidden	Access denied (RBAC, policy)
404 Not Found	Resource not found
409 Conflict	Duplicate or already exists
500 Internal Server Error	Platform error

Best Practices:

- Use Retry-After header for handling 429 (throttling)
- Log correlationId for support or diagnostics
- Use exponential backoff for retries

SDK Usage Patterns

.NET EXAMPLE – CREATE VM:

```
var credentials = SdkContext.AzureCredentialsFactory

.FromServicePrincipal(clientId, clientSecret, tenantId, AzureEnvironment.AzureGlobalCloud);

var azure = Azure.Configure()

.Authenticate(credentials)

.WithSubscription(subscriptionId);
```

```
var vm = azure.VirtualMachines.Define("vm1")
.WithRegion(Region.UKSouth)
.WithNewResourceGroup("rg1")
.WithNewPrimaryNetwork("10.0.0.0/24")
.WithPrimaryPrivateIPAddressDynamic()
.WithNewPrimaryPublicIPAddress("vm1-ip")
.WithPopularLinuxImage(KnownLinuxVirtualMachineImage.UbuntuSer
.WithRootUsername("adminuser")
.WithSsh("ssh-rsa AAAA...")
.WithSize(VirtualMachineSizeTypes.StandardB2ms)
.Create();
```

Python Example – List Resource Groups:

```
from azure.identity import DefaultAzureCredential
from azure.mgmt.resource import ResourceManagementClient
credential = DefaultAzureCredential()
client = ResourceManagementClient(credential, subscription_id)
for rg in client.resource_groups.list():
print(rg.name)
```

Summary

THIS API REFERENCE Guide provides essential examples and patterns to help you interact with Azure programmatically—whether through REST, SDKs, or automation tooling. Knowing these interfaces is critical for DevOps pipelines, backend integration, and custom monitoring or governance systems.

Key Takeaways:

- Use Azure AD for token-based authentication with most management APIs
- Familiarize yourself with request structure, headers, and versioning
- Leverage the Azure SDKs for rapid development in your preferred language
- Handle errors gracefully with retry logic and correlation IDs
- Use APIs not just for automation but to validate architectural decisions

In the next section, we'll explore frequently asked questions that address common exam doubts, certification logistics, and real-world Azure design issues faced by architects.

Frequently Asked Questions

THIS SECTION CONSOLIDATES common questions and detailed answers around the AZ-305 certification, exam logistics, Azure architectural practices, study planning, troubleshooting, and post-certification pathways. Each FAQ addresses real concerns and confusions faced by professionals pursuing the Azure Solutions

Architect Expert certification, and provides clarity with actionable insights.

General Certification FAQs

Q: WHAT IS THE AZ-305 exam and what certification does it contribute to?

A: AZ-305, officially titled *Designing Microsoft Azure Infrastructure Solutions*, is a requirement for earning the **Microsoft Certified: Azure Solutions Architect Expert** credential. Candidates must pass AZ-305 and hold a prerequisite certification such as **AZ-104: Azure Administrator Associate** to receive the expert designation.

Q: How much does the AZ-305 exam cost?

A: As of writing, the AZ-305 exam costs **USD $165**, but pricing may vary by region. Volume licensing or corporate vouchers may reduce the cost.

Q: How long is the AZ-305 exam and how many questions are there?

A: The exam duration is approximately **100–120 minutes** with **40–60 questions**, including multiple-choice, drag-and-drop, case studies, and hot area questions.

Q: What is the passing score for AZ-305?

A: The passing score is **700 out of 1000**. Microsoft uses scaled scoring, so scores do not directly map to percentage of questions answered correctly.

Q: How long is the certification valid?

A: Azure certifications are valid for **one year**. Microsoft provides a free, open-book **renewal assessment** that must be completed before expiration to maintain the credential.

Study Planning and Preparation

Q: HOW LONG SHOULD I study for AZ-305?

A: Depending on experience, most candidates spend **4–8 weeks** preparing. Daily study time of **1–2 hours**, with **practice labs** and **mock exams**, ensures balanced retention and skill development.

Q: What is the best study path if I'm starting from scratch?

A: Suggested path:

1. Complete AZ-104 to build foundational admin knowledge.
2. Begin AZ-305 Learning Paths on Microsoft Learn.
3. Deploy real Azure workloads (e.g., web apps, VNets, backups).
4. Join study groups or online communities (e.g., TechCommunity, Reddit).
5. Practice 2–3 case studies and take a full-length mock exam.

Q: What are some common mistakes during AZ-305 preparation?

A:

- Over-focusing on technical minutiae and ignoring architectural trade-offs.

- Neglecting topics like governance, monitoring, and business continuity.

- Skipping hands-on experience.
- Ignoring Microsoft Learn paths and relying only on video courses.

Exam Logistics and Environment

Q: CAN I TAKE AZ-305 online?

A: Yes. AZ-305 is available through **online proctoring** or at **Pearson VUE test centers.** Online proctoring requires a clean, quiet room with a webcam, microphone, and stable internet connection.

Q: What ID is required?

A: One **government-issued photo ID** is mandatory. The name must match your Microsoft/Certiport profile.

Q: What if I lose internet during the exam?

A: If the session disconnects briefly, it often resumes automatically. For long outages, the exam may be voided and rescheduled via Pearson VUE support.

Q: What if I fail the exam? Can I retake it?

A: Yes. You may retake the exam **after 24 hours** the first time. For subsequent attempts, there is a **14-day waiting period**. There is no limit to retakes, but each attempt requires payment.

Q: Are breaks allowed during the exam?

A: No breaks are permitted in the standard 120-minute AZ-305 session. Time continues to run during any pause.

Technical and Content-Specific Questions

Q: DO I NEED TO MEMORIZE CLI or PowerShell syntax?

A: No. AZ-305 is **architecture-focused**, not operations-focused. You should understand **what a command accomplishes**, not its exact syntax. CLI and PowerShell skills are more relevant for AZ-104 or AZ-700.

Q: What's the difference between Azure Policy and Blueprints?

A:

- **Azure Policy**: Enforces rules on resources (e.g., allowed SKUs, tag requirements).
- **Blueprints**: A packaging mechanism for **Policy**, **RBAC**, **ARM templates**, and **resource groups** for consistent environment provisioning.

Q: When do I use Azure Front Door vs Application Gateway vs Load Balancer?

A:

- **Front Door**: Global routing (layer 7), SSL offloading, WAF, CDN integration.
- **Application Gateway**: Regional layer 7 load balancing with WAF.
- **Load Balancer**: Layer 4 (TCP/UDP) routing, ideal for IaaS workloads.

Q: What is the best Azure service for running microservices?

A: Use **Azure Kubernetes Service (AKS)** for container orchestration with full control. Alternatively, use **Azure Container Apps** or **Functions** for simpler event-driven architectures.

Q: Can I bring my own public IP addresses to Azure?

A: Yes. Azure supports **BYOIP** for public IP ranges in specific scenarios, mainly for enterprises with strict routing or regulatory requirements.

Post-Certification and Career Guidance

Q: I PASSED AZ-305. What next?

A:

- Ensure AZ-104 (or equivalent) is complete to earn **Azure Solutions Architect Expert.**
- Add the certification to your **LinkedIn profile**, **resume**, and **job portals.**
- Seek out projects involving real Azure architectures.
- Explore next certifications like **AZ-400** (DevOps) or **SC-100** (Security Architect).

Q: Will this certification help me get a job as a Cloud Architect?

A: Yes, but it's just one part of the equation. Real-world project experience, soft skills, and a demonstrable portfolio (e.g., GitHub repos, solution diagrams) are also essential. AZ-305 validates you can design scalable, secure, cost-optimized solutions in Azure.

Q: How do I maintain my knowledge after certification?

A:

- Follow **Azure Updates** (https://azure.microsoft.com/en-us/updates/)
- Subscribe to **Architectural Decision Guides** and **Azure Friday** YouTube channel

- Attend conferences like **Microsoft Build**, **Ignite**, and **Global Azure Bootcamp**
- Practice building solutions in your personal Azure tenant or sandbox accounts

---

Advanced Questions from Experienced Professionals

Q: CAN I AUTOMATE EVERYTHING covered in AZ-305 with Terraform or Bicep?

A: Nearly all infrastructure and governance patterns in AZ-305 can be automated with **Terraform**, **ARM**, or **Bicep**. Certain identity configurations and monitoring alerts may require additional scripting or manual review for compliance.

Q: How do I approach multi-tenant SaaS architecture in Azure?

A:

- Use **App Service** with per-tenant resource isolation or **shared hosting with RBAC**
- Manage user access through **Azure AD B2C**
- Use **Cosmos DB** or **SQL Elastic Pools** for tenant data isolation
- Implement **Front Door + APIM** for unified routing and API management

Q: How can I model complex access and identity requirements across multiple Azure tenants?

A:

- Use **Azure Lighthouse** for delegated resource management

- Combine with **RBAC**, **Conditional Access**, and **Privileged Identity Management**
- Use **Management Groups** to enforce policies across tenants with consolidated billing/reporting

Q: How do I monitor for configuration drift across environments?

A:

- Use **Azure Policy compliance scans** with **non-compliant resource reporting**
- Combine with **Azure Resource Graph** for querying drift
- Use **Terraform state** comparison tools for IaC environments

---

Summary

THESE FREQUENTLY ASKED questions are based on years of exam experience, real Azure architecture consultations, and interactions with certification candidates. Addressing them ensures that you're not only prepared to pass the AZ-305 exam but also positioned to thrive as a modern cloud architect.

Final Takeaways:

- Focus on learning outcomes, not just passing scores
- Use Microsoft Learn, real projects, and community support to grow
- Don't memorize—**understand the "why"** behind each design decision

- Follow a lifelong learning approach with continuous experimentation
- Think architecturally, design with empathy for the business, and build resiliently

With this, you now have a complete preparation companion—from exam readiness to real-world execution. The cloud moves fast—but with the foundation you've built through this guide, so will you.

www.ingramcontent.com/pod-product-compliance
Lightning Source LLC
LaVergne TN
LVHW090302210926
848480LV00001B/100